HAL•LEONARD

LISTEN ONLINE

PREVIEW AUDIO CLIPS

PIANO • VOCAL • GUITAR

THE Bride's WEDDING MUSIC COLLECTION

ISBN 978-1-4584-1548-6

HAL•LEONARD® CORPORATION

7777 W. BLUEMOUND RD. P.O. BOX 13819 MILWAUKEE, WI 53213

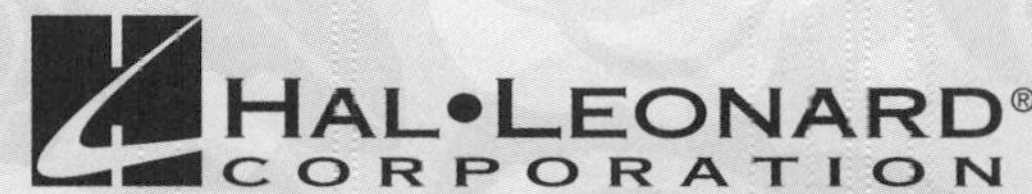

Visit Hal Leonard Online at
www.halleonard.com

CONTENTS BY CATEGORY

PRELUDES & PROCESSIONALS

RECESSIONALS

POP SONGS

COUNTRY SONGS

CONTEMPORARY CHRISTIAN SONGS

HYMNS & SACRED SONGS

ALPHABETICAL LISTING

CANON IN D

By JOHANN PACHELBEL

Adagio

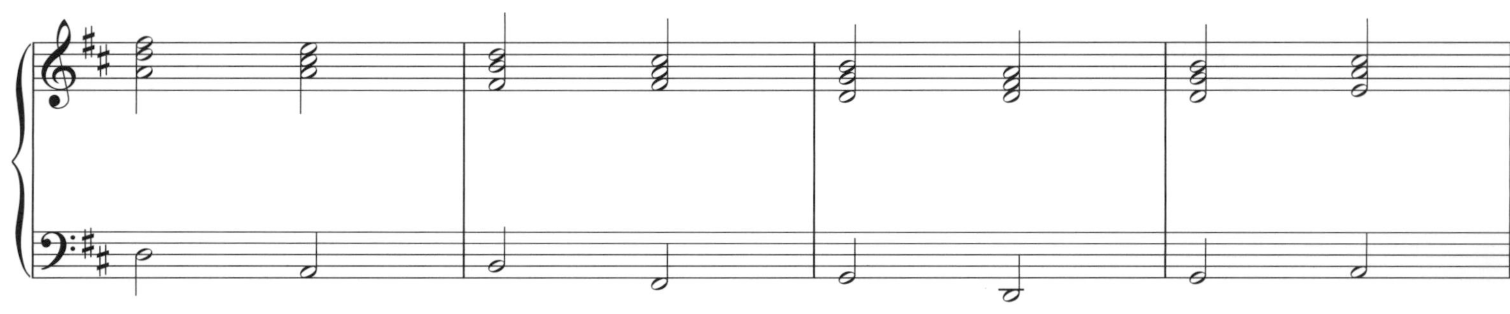

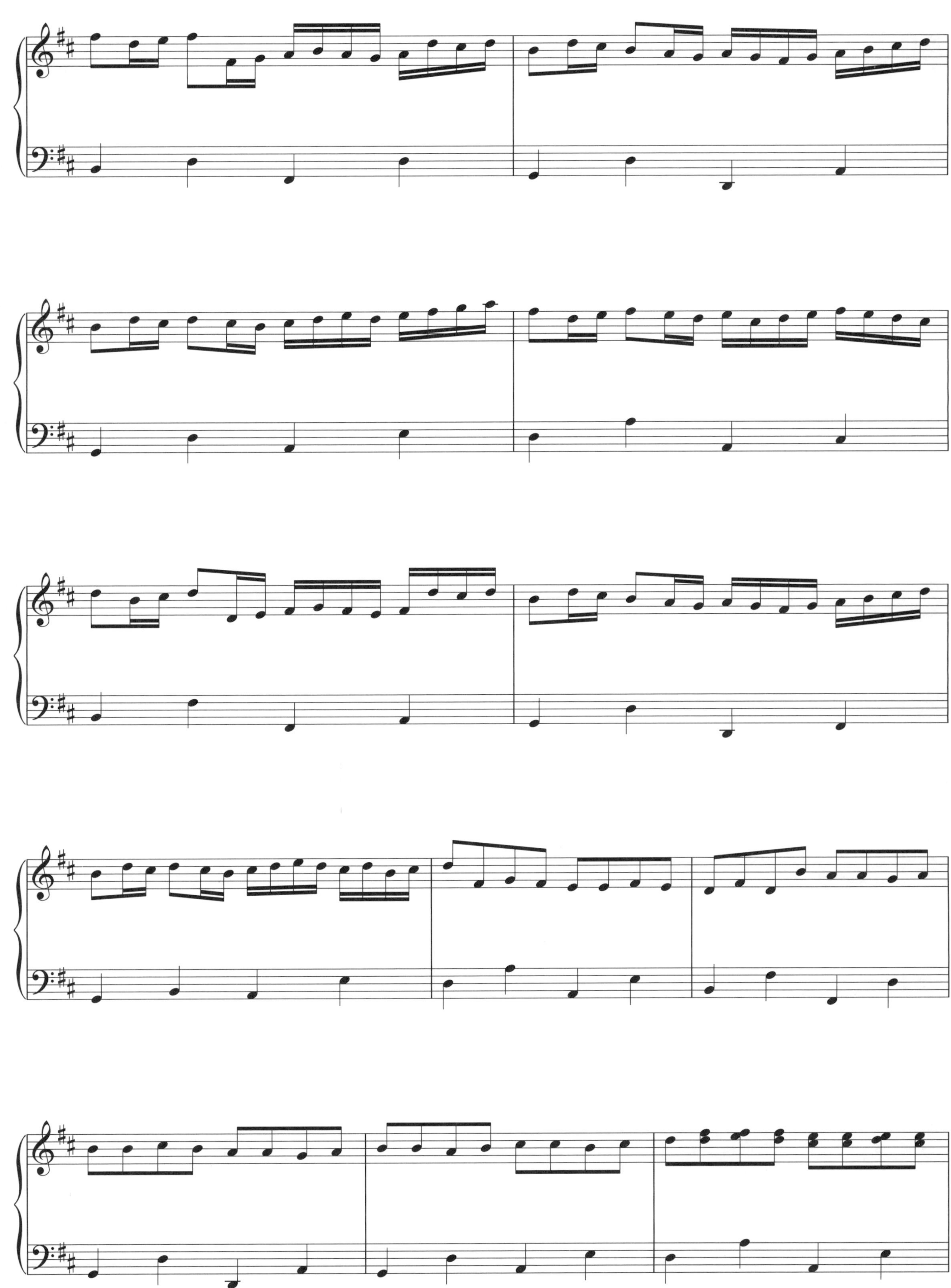

rit.

DAWN
from PRIDE AND PREJUDICE

By DARIO MARIANELLI

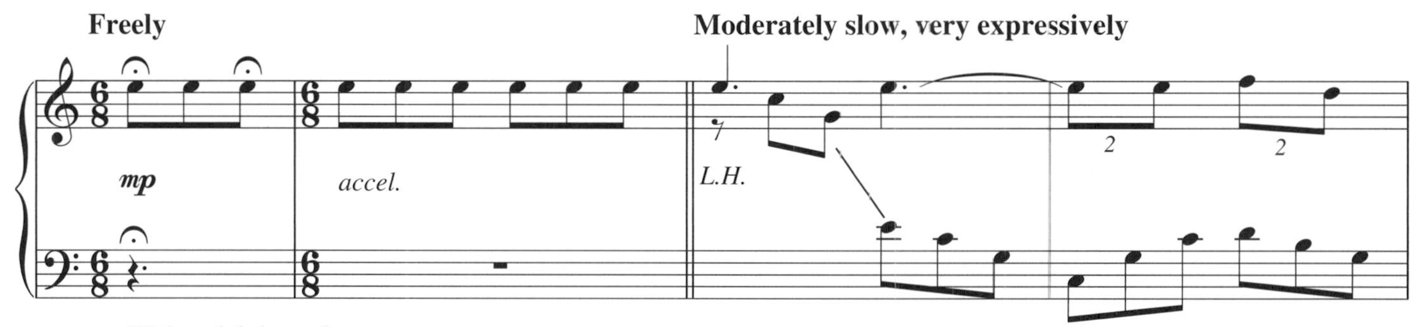
Freely
Moderately slow, very expressively
mp
accel.
L.H.
With pedal throughout

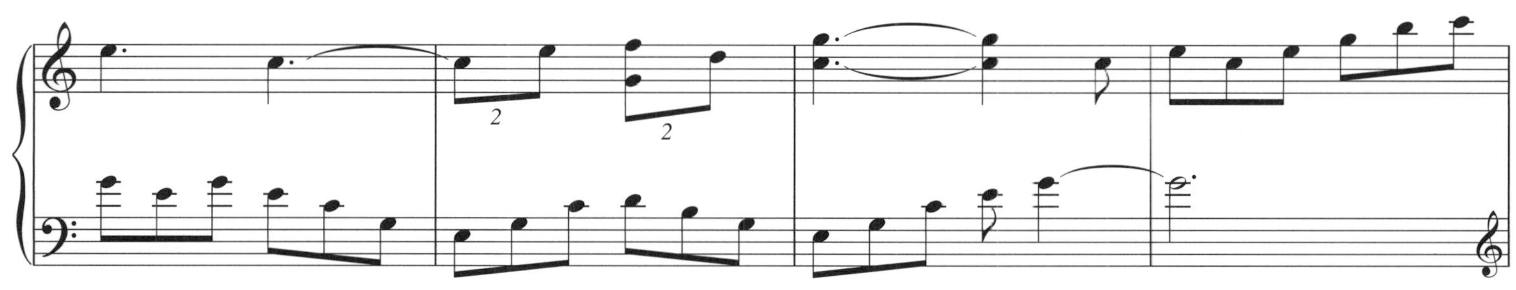

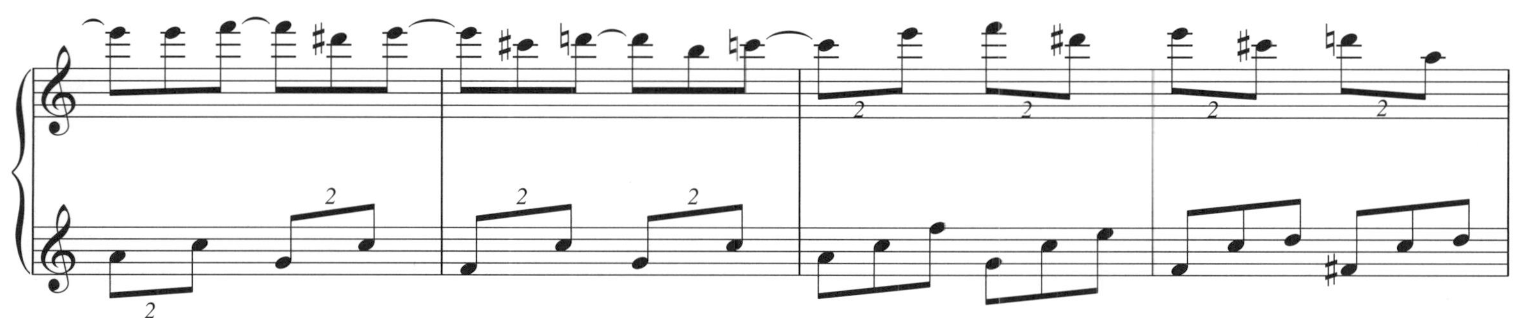

Moderately fast, with motion
rit.

Slightly slower

rit.
Slowly
8va
(8va)
rit.

FOREVER IN LOVE

By KENNY G

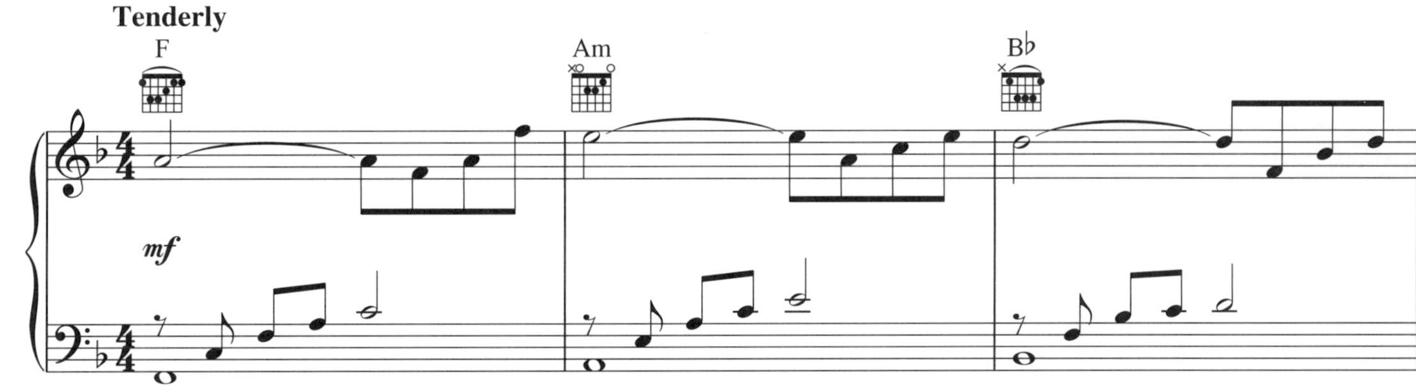

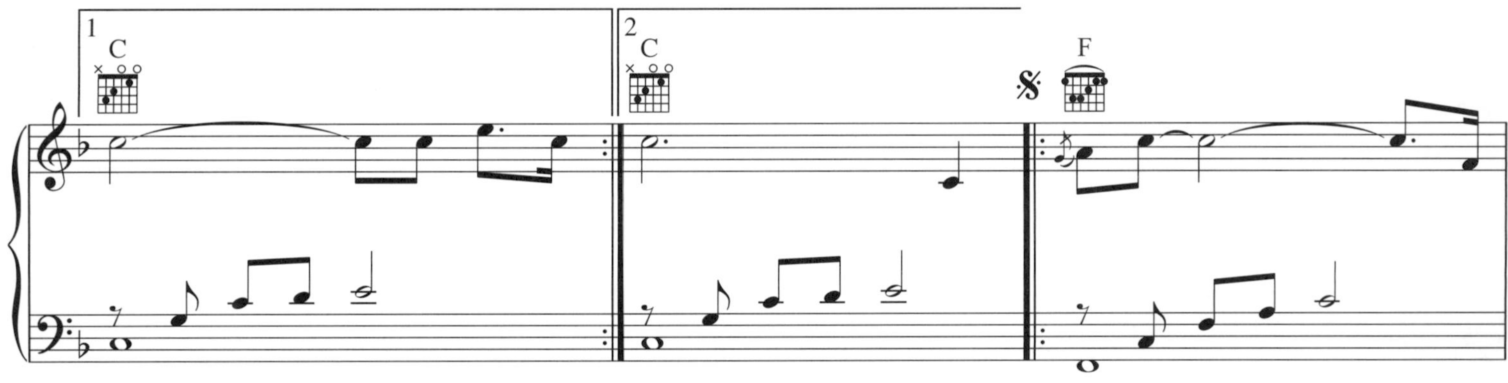

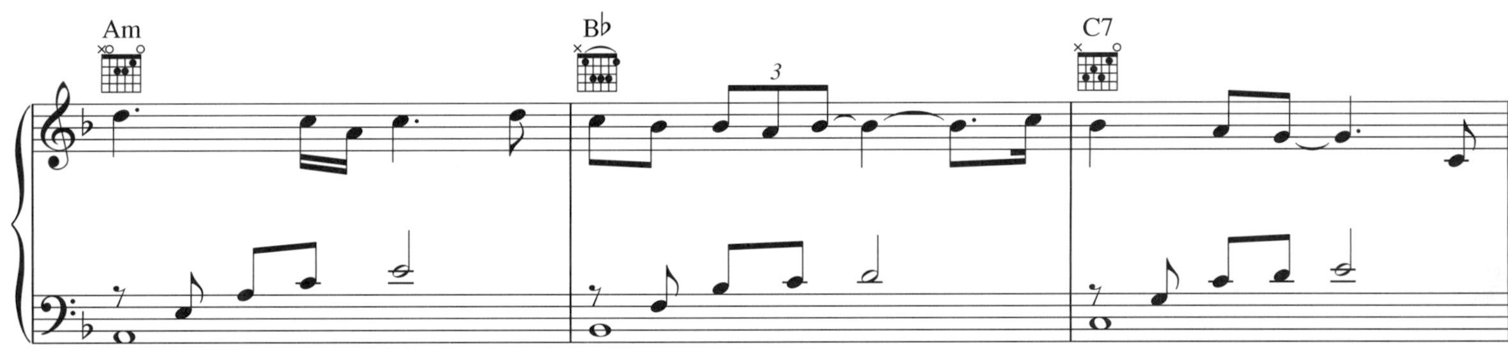

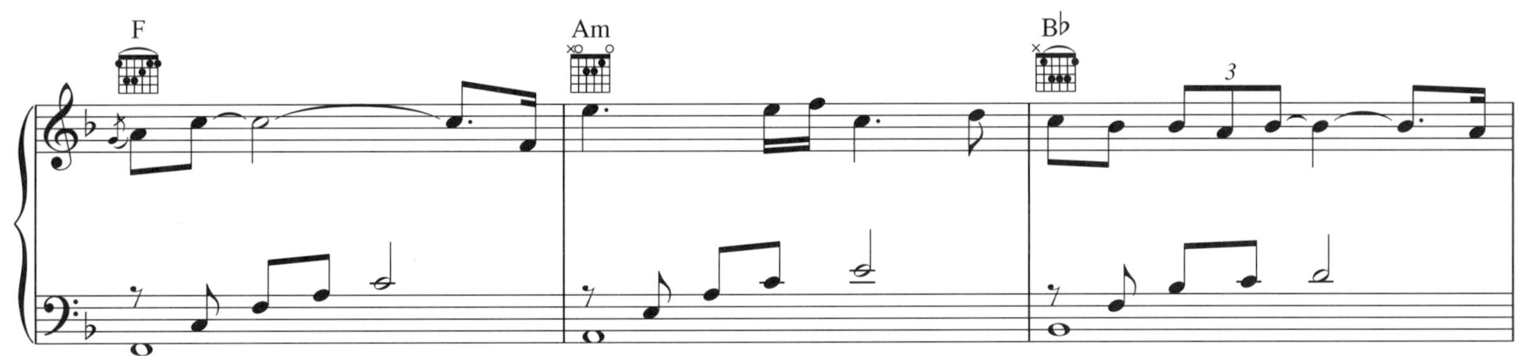

C7
B♭(add2)
3fr
C
Dm
Asus
F(add2)
Am
B♭
C
To Coda
F
1
Am
B♭
C
2
Am
B♭

C
F
Am
B♭
C
F
Am
B♭
C
D.S. al Coda
CODA
F
Am
B♭
C
F
Am

B♭
C
F
Am
B♭
C
F
Am
B♭
C
F
Am
mp
B♭
C
F(add2)
rit.

Highland Cathedral

By MICHAEL KORB
and ULRICH ROEVER

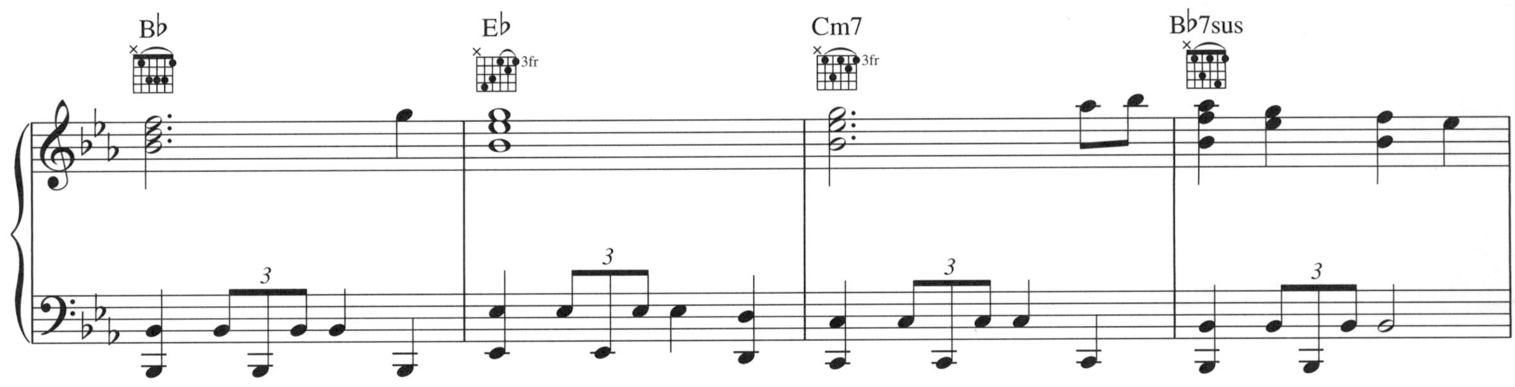

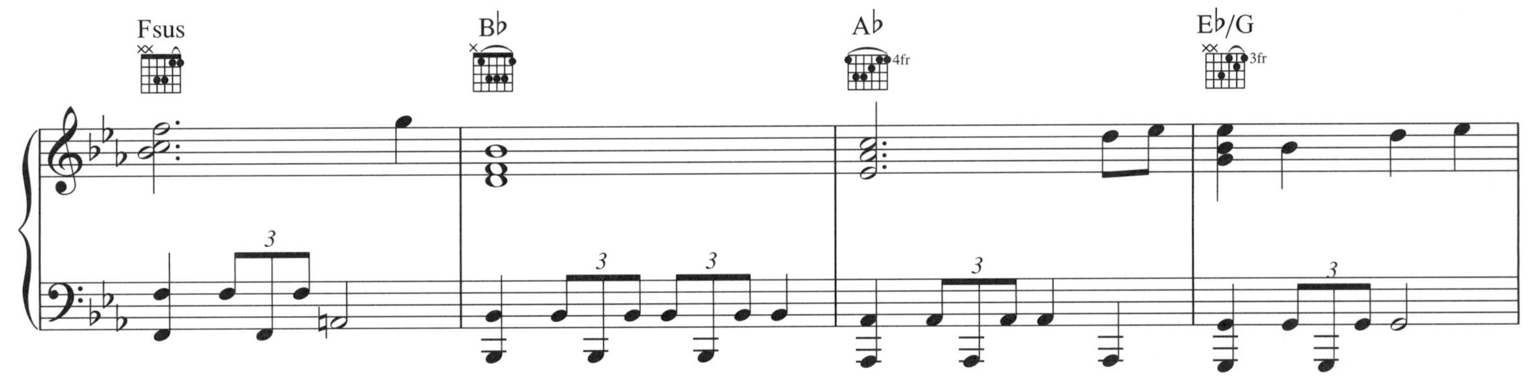

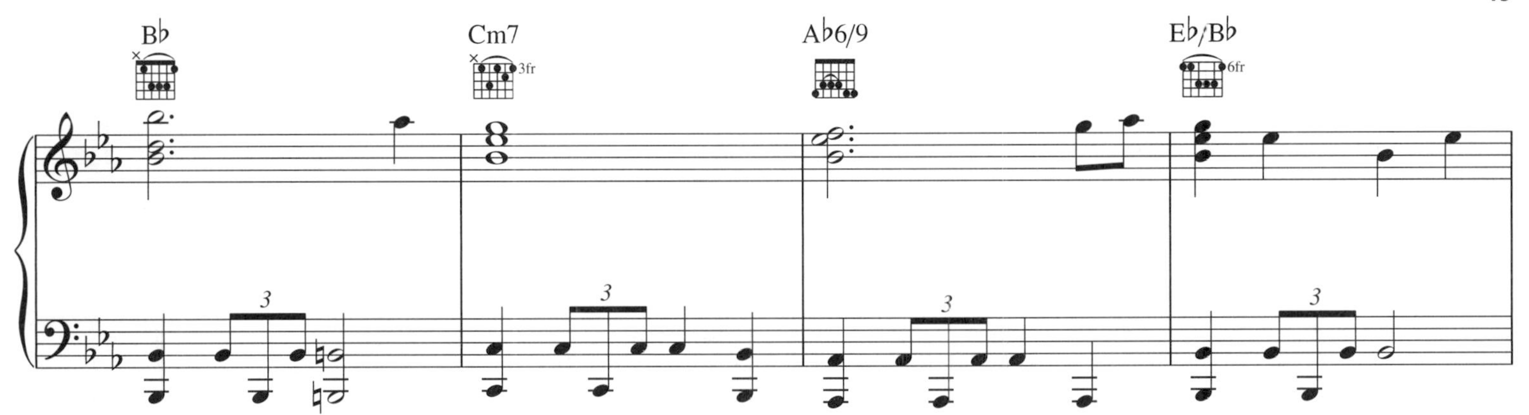
B♭
Cm7
3fr
A♭6/9
E♭/B♭
6fr
3

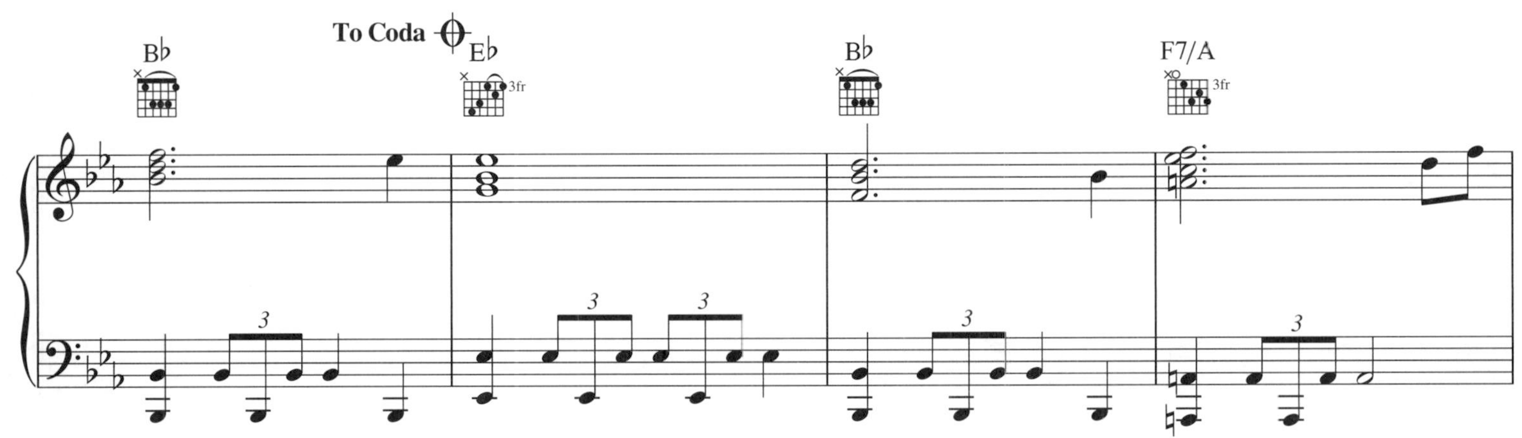
To Coda
B♭
E♭
3fr
B♭
F7/A
3fr
3

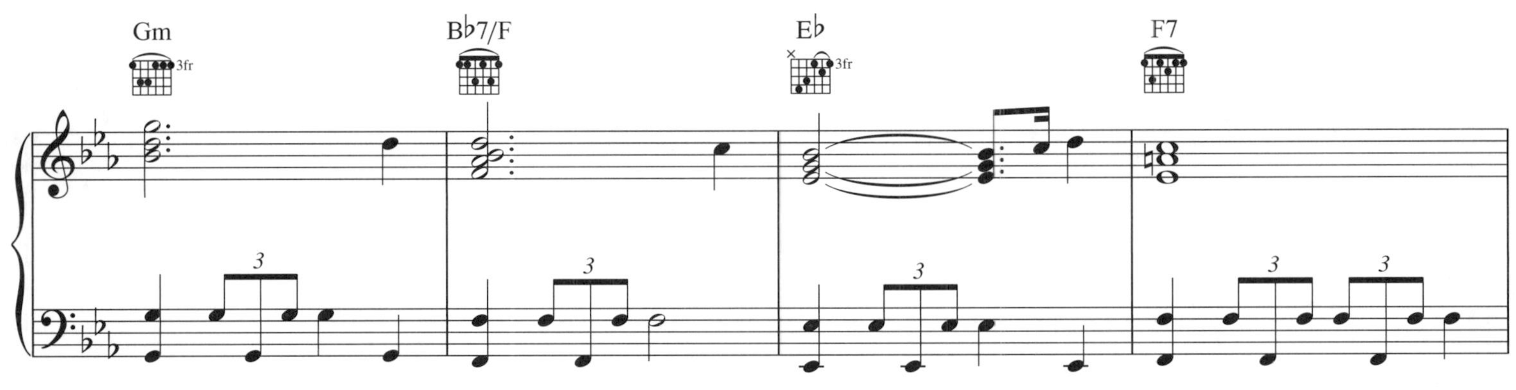
Gm
3fr
B♭7/F
E♭
3fr
F7
3

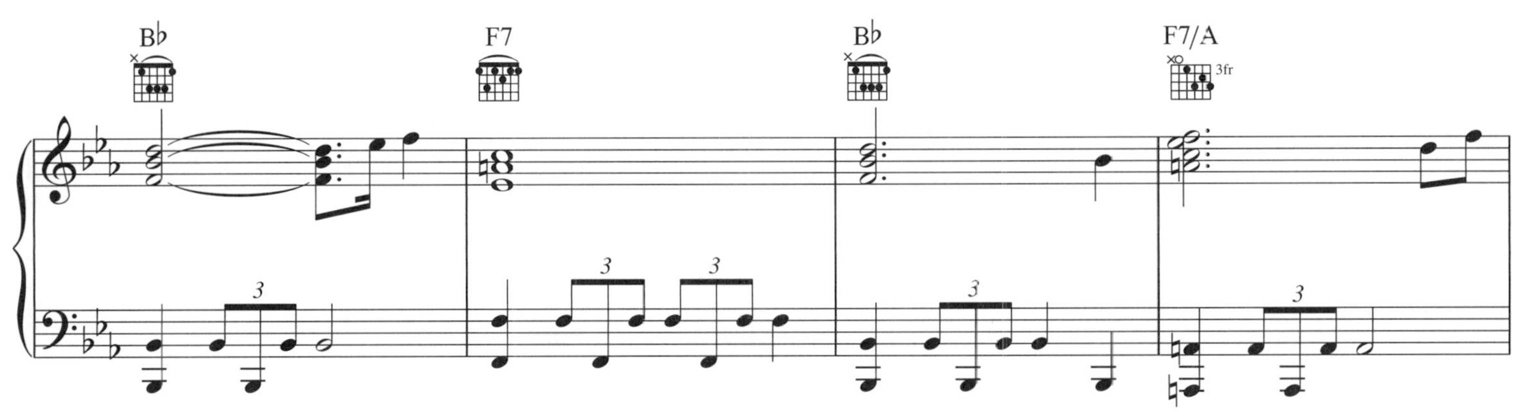
B♭
F7
B♭
F7/A
3fr
3

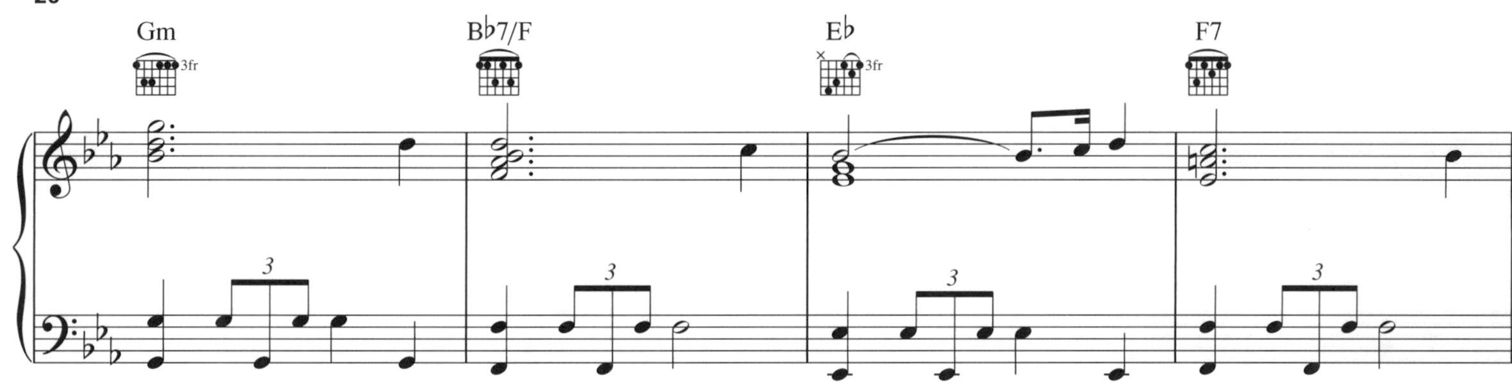
Gm
3fr
B♭7/F
E♭
3fr
F7
3
3
3
3

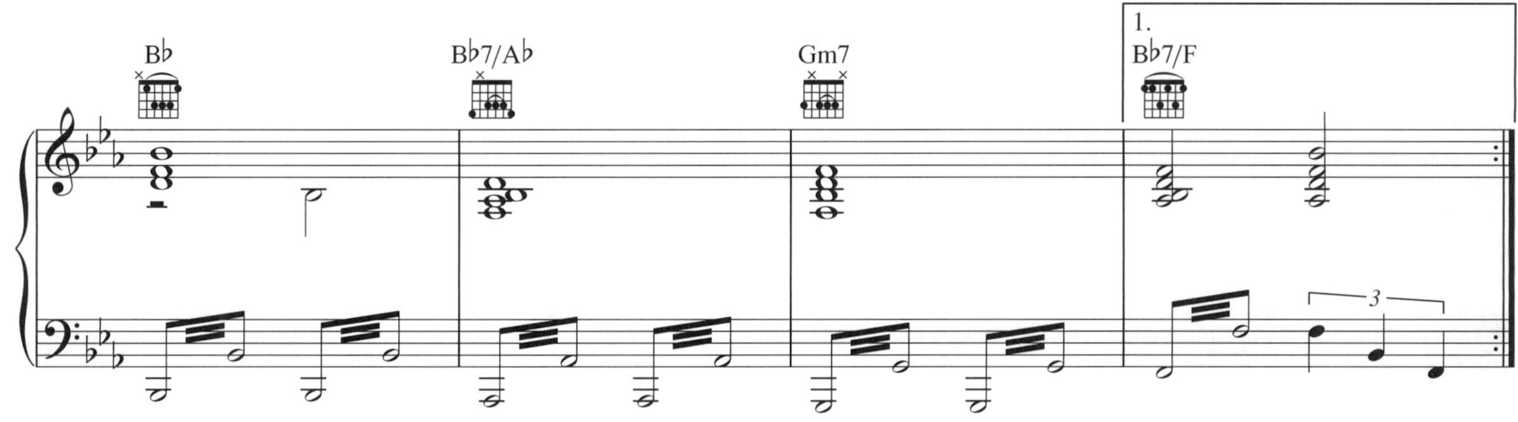
B♭
B♭7/A♭
Gm7
1.
B♭7/F
3

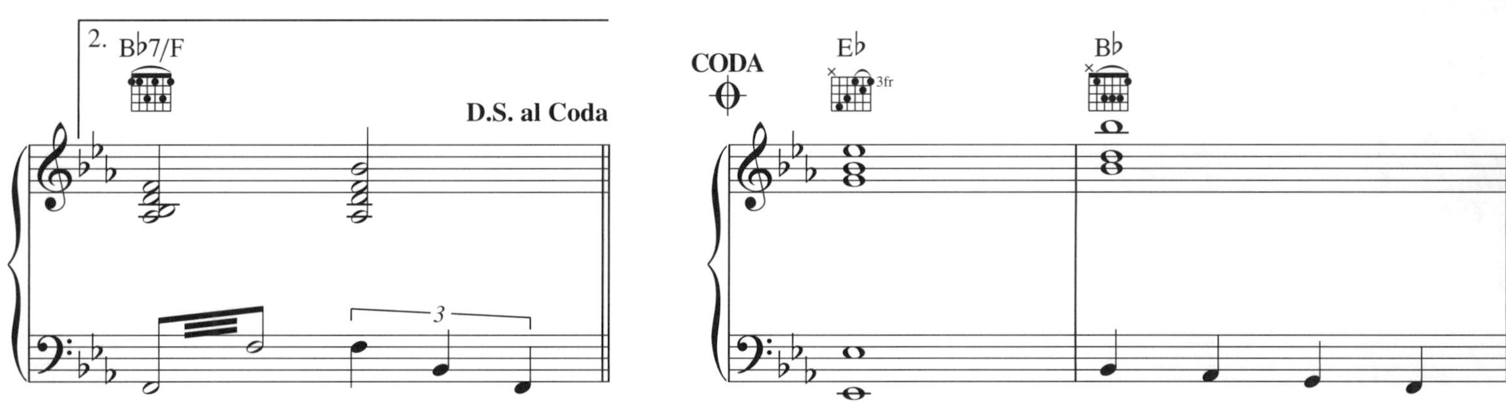
2. B♭7/F
D.S. al Coda
3
CODA
E♭
3fr
B♭

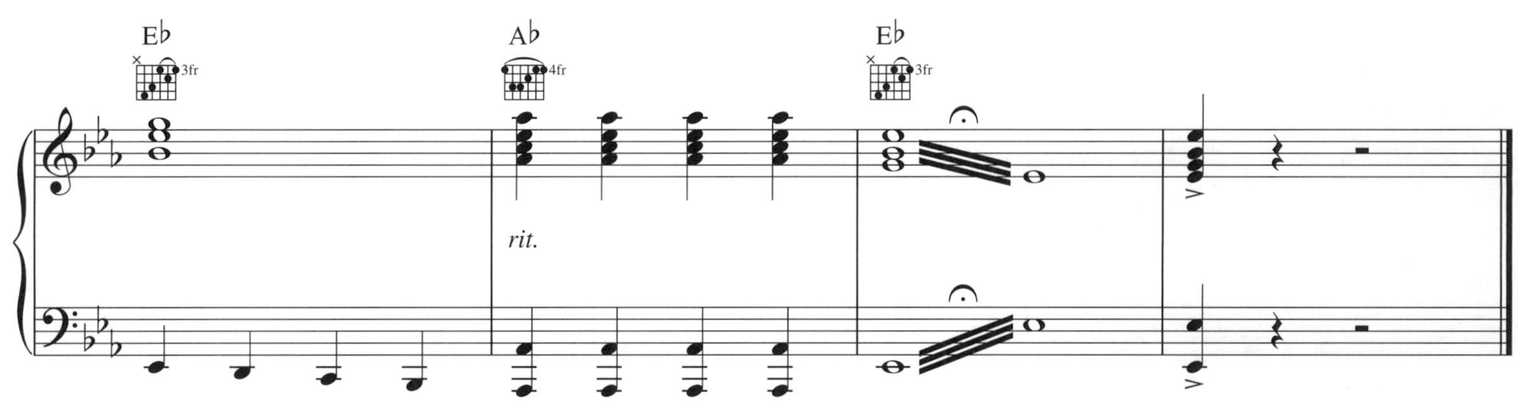
E♭
3fr
A♭
4fr
E♭
3fr
rit.

JESU, JOY OF MAN'S DESIRING

from CANTATA NO. 147

English Words by ROBERT BRIDGES
Music by JOHANN SEBASTIAN BACH

G/B
Em
C
Bm/D
D7
G
C/E
wis - dom, love most bright,
peace - ful mu - sic rings,
G/B
Em
Am
G/B
C
D
G
C/E
G/B
Em
C6
D7
G
C/E
D/F♯
Em7
Bm/D
Drawn by Thee, our
Where the flock in
C/E
D/F♯
G
D
G
C/E
souls as - pir - ing,
Thee con - fid - ing,
Soar to
Drink of

G/B
Em
C
Bm/D
D7
G
C/E
un - cre - at - ed light.
joy from death - less springs.
G/B
Em
Am
G/B
C
D
G
C/E
G/B
Em
C
D7
G
D
G♯dim/B
Am
Bm7♭5
E7
Am
Dm/F
Word of God our flesh that fash - ioned,
Theirs is beau - ty's fair - est pleas - ure,

Am/C
Fmaj7
Am/E
Dm
D♯dim
6fr
E7
Am
G/B
With the
Theirs is
C
Dm
G7
C
C7
F
G7/B
fire of life ___ im - pas - sioned.
wis - dom's ho - liest treas - ure.
C
G
C/E
G/B
Em7
Am
G/B
C
Striv - ing still to truth un -
Thou dost ev - er lead Thine
D
D7
G
C/E
known,
own,
Soar - ing
In the

G/B
Em
C
Bm/D
D7
G
dy - ing round Thy throne.
love of joys un - known.
G7
Am/G
F♯dim/G
G
G6
D7/G
G
C/E
G/B
Em
Am
G/B
C
D
G
C/E
G/B
Em
C6
D7
1
G
2
G

Prelude in C Major
from THE WELL-TEMPERED CLAVIER, BOOK 1

By JOHANN SEBASTIAN BACH

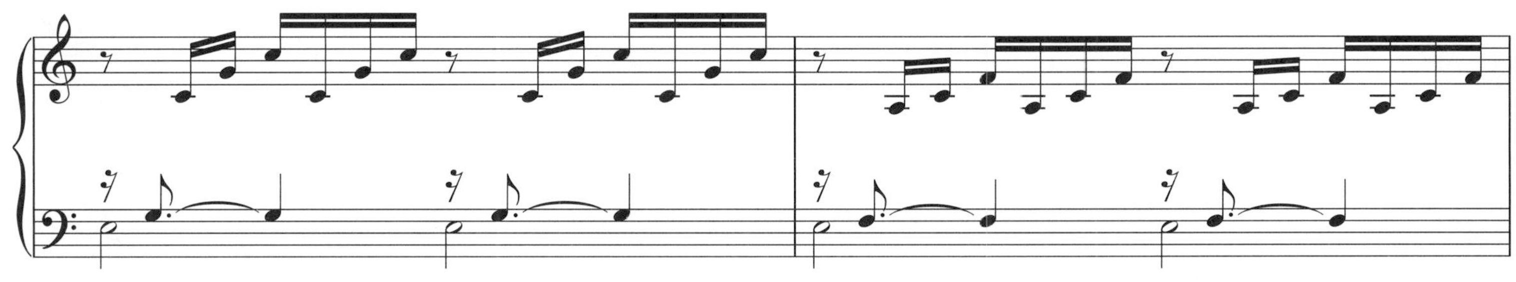

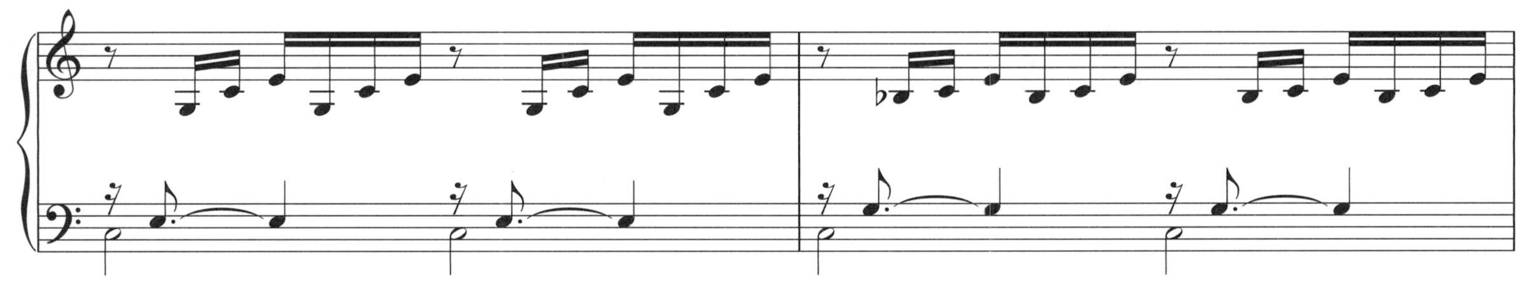

TRUMPET VOLUNTARY

By JEREMIAH CLARKE

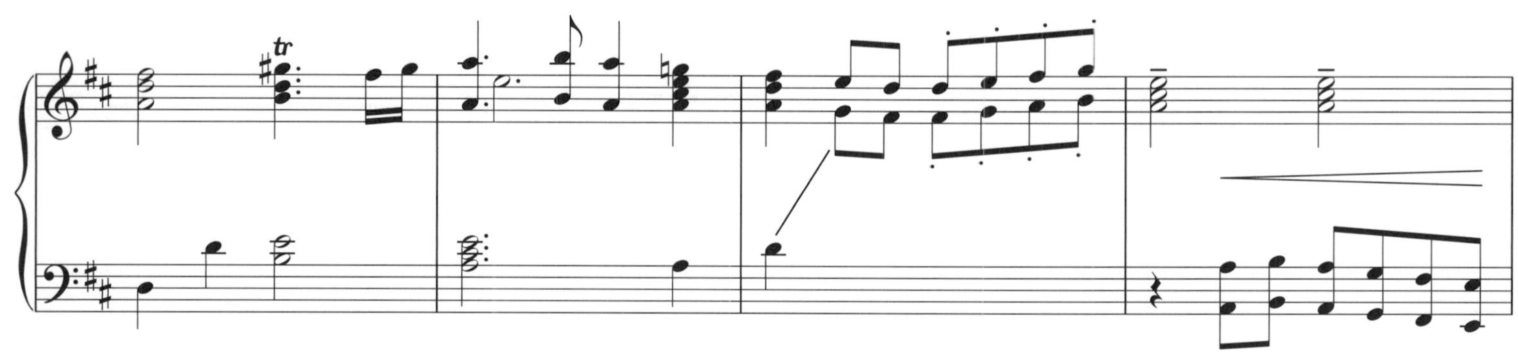

tr
ff

tr
tr

f

ff

p

tr
ff

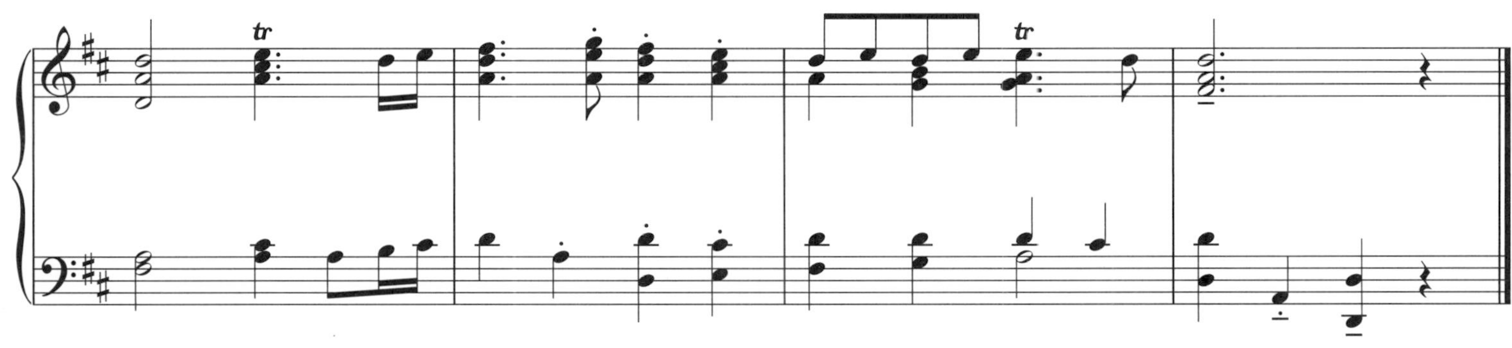
tr
tr

Wedding Processional

from THE SOUND OF MUSIC

Lyrics by OSCAR HAMMERSTEIN II
Music by RICHARD RODGERS

For the entrance of the Bride
rit.
a tempo
3

3
ff
rit.

Allegro Maestoso

from WATER MUSIC

By GEORGE FRIDERIC HANDEL

p
mf

p

mf
cresc.

f
mf

p

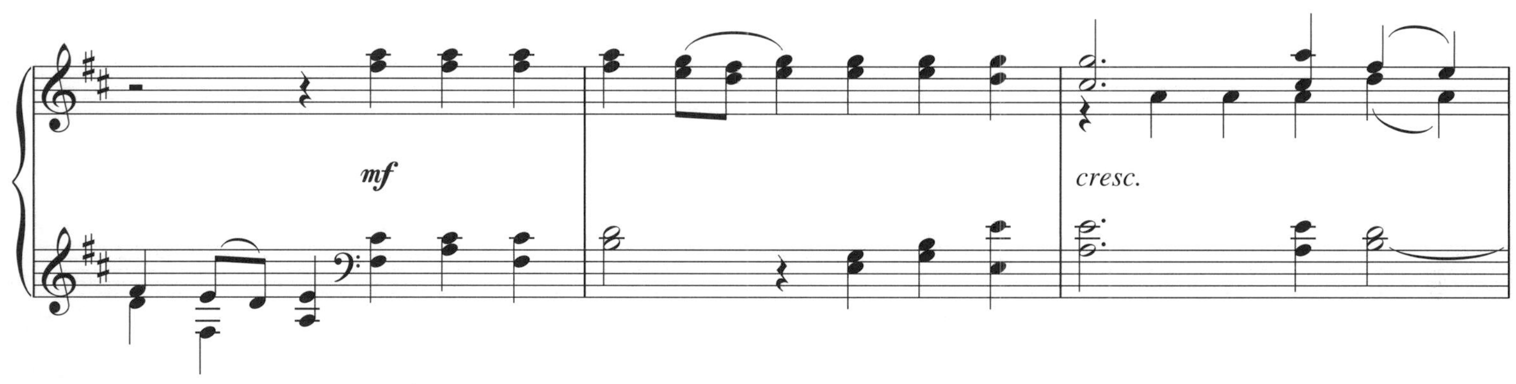
mf
cresc.

tr
f
cresc.

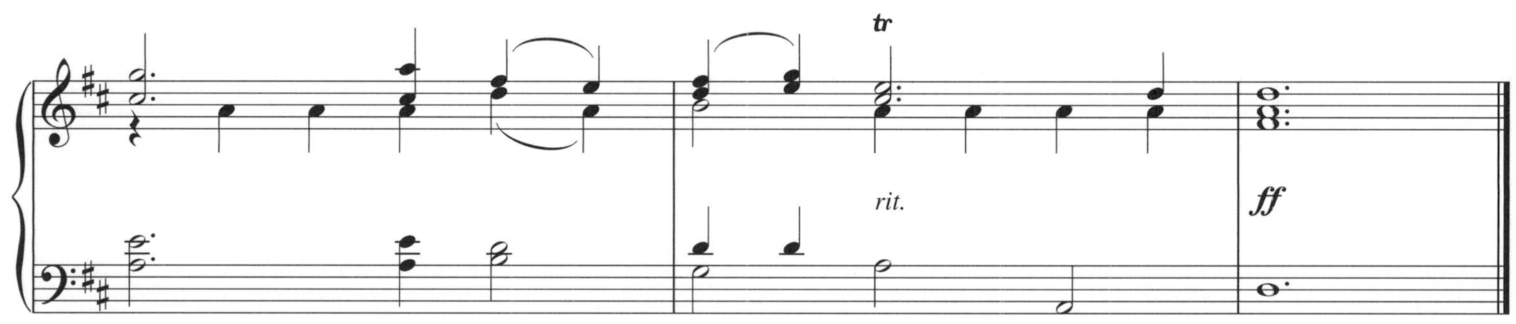
tr
rit.
ff

Ode to Joy

from SYMPHONY NO. 9 IN D MINOR

By LUDWIG VAN BEETHOVEN

With spirit

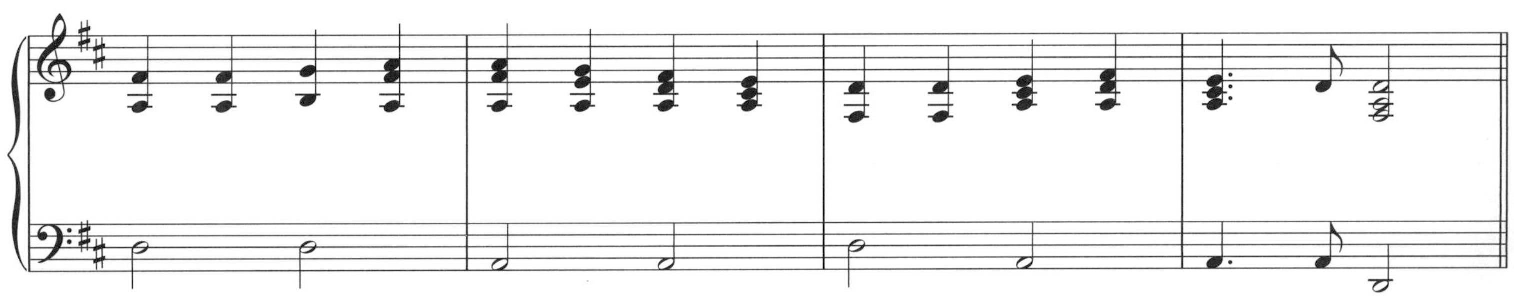

1.
2.

Rondeau
Excerpt

By JEAN-JOSEPH MOURET

cresc.
f
tr
tr
rit.

Trumpet Tune

By HENRY PURCELL

mf

tr

tr
rit.

Wedding March

from A MIDSUMMER NIGHT'S DREAM

By FELIX MENDELSSOHN

Allegro

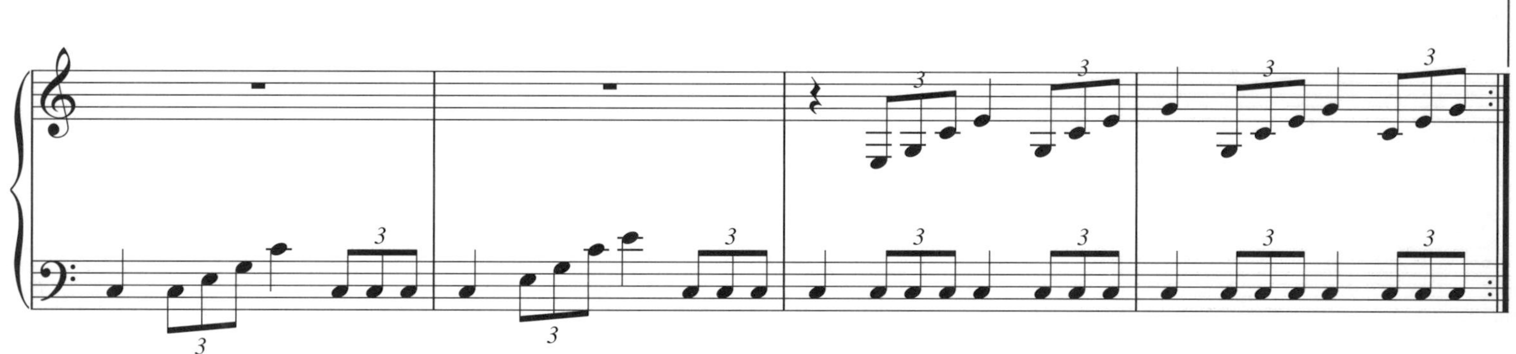

2.
1.
2.
To next strain
Fine
p

p
sf
1.
2.

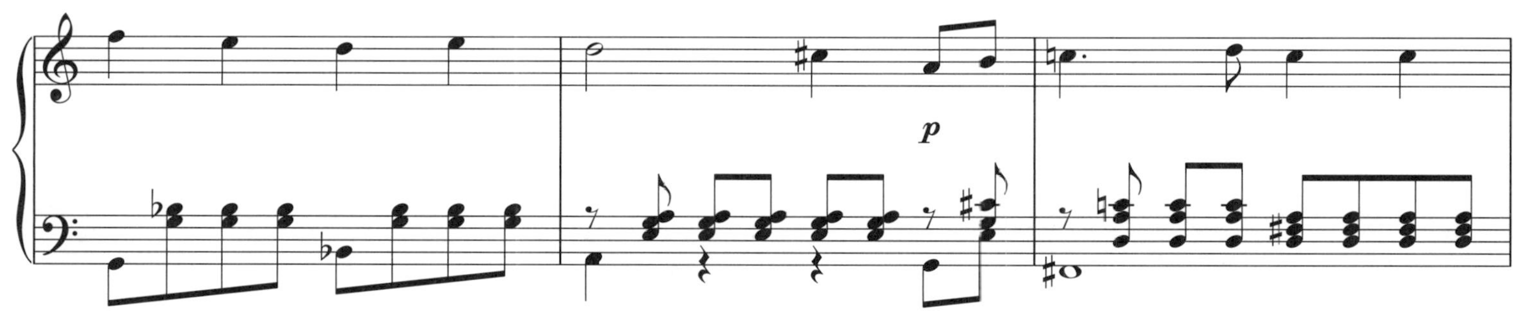

D.S. al Fine

Here and Now

Words and Music by TERRY STEELE
and DAVID ELLIOT

G(add9)/B
B7/D♯
Em7
G/B
Cmaj9
Hold - ing you close through the night, I need you.
C/D
G(add9)
Yeah.
I look in your
I look in your
F♯m7♭5
4fr
B7♭9
Em7
D
eyes, and there I see what
eyes, there I see
C(add9)
C/D
G(add9)
hap - pi - ness real - ly means. The love that we
all that a love should real - ly be. And I need you

F♯m7♭5
B7♭9
Cmaj7
G/B
share makes life so sweet. To -
more and more each day.
C(add9)/E
Cm6/E♭
G/D
C(add9)
geth - er we'll al - ways be.
Noth - ing can take your love a - way.
G(add9)/B
B7/D♯
Em7
G/B
This pledge of love feels so right, and, ooh, I need
More than I dare to dream. I need
Cmaj9
F♯m7♭5
A/B
Cmaj9
you. Yeah.
you.
Here and now,

D/C
D/F♯
G
G/B
I prom - ise to love faith - ful - ly.
Cmaj9
F♯m7♭5
4fr
A/B
Cmaj9
You're all I need.
Here and now, I
D/C
D/F♯
G
G/B
Cmaj9
To Coda
vow to be one with thee.
1
C
C/D
G
G/B
C
C/D
Your love is all I need.
Stay.

G(add9)
G/B
C
C/D
2
C
C/D
When Your love is all I
Cmaj9
D/C
D
need. Start-ing here, ooh, and I'm start - ing now. I be-lieve.
G
Cmaj9
Start - ing here, I'm start - ing right here. Start - ing now,
(I be - lieve.)
C/D
right now, be-cause I be - lieve in your love, so I'm

F/G
G/B
Cmaj9
D.S. al Coda
glad to take the vow. Here and now, oh, I
CODA
C
C/D
G(add9)
Your love is all I, I, yeah,
need. Vocal ad lib.
G(add9)/B
Cmaj9
1, 2
B♭maj9
Cmaj9
Fmaj9
yeah. Uh, yeah. Ay ah, love is all I
last time: rit.
3
B♭maj9
C(add9)
G(add9)
Yeah.

I Have and Always Will

Words and Music by
DAVE BARNES

D♭
A♭
4fr
All of these friends here a - gree,
This is a big mys - ter - y
D♭
D♭m6
we're right where we should be.
how I found you found me.
A♭
4fr
E♭/G
3fr
Fm
Un - der - neath all
D♭
A♭
4fr
E♭sus/G
3fr
your white,
my

Fm
D♭
E♭sus
6fr
E♭
3fr
la - dy, my love, my bride,
D♭
A♭
4fr
in your dark - est ho - urs
D♭
A♭
4fr
D♭
will I love you still, I have and I
A♭/E♭
E♭7
1
A♭
4fr
D♭maj7
al - ways will.

2
A♭
D♭maj7
4fr
I will.
E♭
3fr
And you are chang - ing now,
B♭m7
you're part of me some - how,
and I will
nev - er be a - lone.
In

D♭
A♭
4fr
D♭
your dark - est ho - urs will I love you still,
A♭
4fr
D♭
A♭/E♭
Edim7
I have and I al - ways
Fm
B♭7sus
B♭7
D♭
will.
I have and I
A♭/E♭
E♭7
A♭
4fr
A♭sus
4fr
D♭m6
D♭m6/F♭
A♭(add2)/E♭
al - ways will.
rit.

EVERYTHING

Words and Music by AMY FOSTER-GILLIES,
MICHAEL BUBLÉ and ALAN CHANG

Moderately fast
D
Bm7
E7
G6
Asus
mp
Gm(maj7)
Gm6/A
3fr
D5
5fr
A7sus
You're a fall - in' star, you're the get - a - way car, you're the line in the sand when I go
ou - sel, you're a wish - ing well, and you light me up when you ring
G
A7(add4)

D
A7sus
D
Bm7
too far. You're the swim - ming pool on an Au -
my bell. You're a mys - ter - y, you're from out -
E7
G
A7(add4)
3fr
gust day, and you're the per - fect thing to say.
er space, you're ev - 'ry min - ute of my ev - 'ry day.
D
A7sus
D
Bm7
And you play it coy, but it's kind
And I can't be - lieve, oh, that I'm
E7
Gm
3fr
Gm6/A
3fr
of cute. When you smile at me, you know ex - act - ly
your man, and I get to kiss you, ba - by, just be -

D
A7sus
D
Bm7
what you do. Ba - by, don't pre - tend that you don't know
cause I can. What - ev - er comes our way, oh, we'll see
E7
Gm
Gm6/A
3fr
3fr
it's true, 'cause you can see it when I look at you.
it through. And you know that's what our love can do.
D
G
A6
D
Bm7
And in this cra - zy life, and through these
G
A6
D
D7
cra - zy times, it's you, it's you.

G
F♯
Bm
Bm/A
E7
You make me sing.
You're ev - 'ry line,
you're ev - 'ry word,
1
Gm(maj7)
3fr
Gm6/A
3fr
D
Bm7
E7
you're ev - 'ry - thing.
Gm(maj7)
3fr
Gm6/A
3fr
D5
5fr
A7sus
You're a car -
2
Gm(maj7)
3fr
Gm6/A
3fr
you're ev - 'ry - thing.
D
Bm7
E7
Gm(maj7)
3fr
Gm6/A
3fr
Guitar solo ad lib.
(Vocal 1st time only)

1
D5
2
D5
D
Bm7
Solo ends
So la, la,
E7
1
Gm(maj7)
Gm6/A
la, la, la, la, la.
So
2
Gm(maj7) Gm6/A
D5
A
B6
la, la, la. And in this cra - zy life,
E
C♯m7
A
B6
and through these cra - zy times,

E
E7
A
G♯
4fr
C♯m
4fr
C♯m/B
it's you, it's you. You make me sing. You're ev - 'ry line,
F♯7
Am(maj7)
G♯7♯5
4fr
C♯m
4fr
3
you're ev - 'ry word, you're ev - 'ry - thing.
C♯m/B
F♯7
You're ev - 'ry song,
Am(maj7)
Am/B
and I sing a - long 'cause you're my ev - 'ry - thing.

E
C♯m7
4fr
F♯7
A6
Bsus
E
C♯m7
4fr
F♯7
A6
Bsus
E
C♯m7
4fr
F♯7
So la, la, la, la,
Am(maj7)
Am6/B
E
E
C♯m7
4fr
la, la, la.
So la, la,
rit.
F♯7
Am
E5
la, la, la, la, la, la, la, la, la.

MARRY ME

Words and Music by
PAT MONAHAN

Moderately, in 2
C/E
Fsus2
mp
With pedal
C/E
Fsus2
C
For -
To -
Gsus/B
G/B
ev - er could nev - er be long e - nough _ for me _____ to
geth - er can nev - er be close e - nough _ for me _____ to

Am7
Gsus
3fr
Fsus2
feel like I've had long e - nough with you.
feel like I am close e - nough to you.
C
For - get the world now,
You wear white, and
Gsus/B
G/B
Am7
we won't let them see. But there's
I'll wear out the words "I love you"
Gsus
3fr
Fsus2
one thing left to do:
and "you're beau - ti - ful."

C/E
Fsus2
Now that the weight has lift - ed,
Now that the wait is o - ver
C/E
love has sure - ly
and love has fi - n'lly
Fsus2
C
shift - ed my way,
showed her my way,
mar - ry me,
Gsus/B
G/B

Am7
Gsus
3fr
Fsus2
to - day and ev - 'ry day.
C
Mar - ry
Gsus/B
G/B
Am7
me.
If I ev - er get the nerve
Gsus
3fr
Fsus2
to say "hel - lo" in this ca -

C/E
fé, say you will,
mm,
Fsus2
C/E
To Coda
say you will,
Fsus2
1
mm.
2
Fsus2/B♭
Prom - ise me

Fsus2/A
C
you'll al - ways be
Gsus/B
G/B
hap - py by my side.
Fsus2/B♭
Fsus2/A
I prom - ise to sing
C
to you
when all the mu - sic

Gsus/B
G/B
Fsus2/B♭
dies.
Fsus2/A
D.S. al Coda
And
CODA
Fsus2
mm,
mar - ry
C/E
Fsus2
me,
mm.

IN MY LIFE

Words and Music by JOHN LENNON
and PAUL McCARTNEY

Moderately
A
E7
A
mp
E7
A
F#m
A7
There are plac - es I'll re - mem - ber all my
But of all these friends and lov - ers there is
D
Dm
A
life, though some have changed. Some for - ev - er, not for
no one com - pares with you. And these mem - 'ries lose their
F#m
A7
D
Dm
A
bet - ter; some have gone and some re - main. All these
mean - ing when I think of love as some - thing new. Tho' I

F♯m D G

(1.) plac - es had their mo - ments with lov - ers and friends I
(2.,3.) know I'll nev - er lose af - fec - tion for peo - ple and things that

A F♯m

still can re - call. Some are dead and some are
went be - fore, I know I'll of - ten stop and think a -

B7 Dm A **To Coda**

liv - ing, in my life I've loved them all.
bout them, in my life I love you more.

N.C.

8va

In 18th century style

(8va)

1

2

D.S. al Coda

Tho' I

(8va)

CODA

A

E7

Dm

N.C.

In my life I love you

slower

A

E7

A

more.

a tempo

NOW AND FOREVER

Words and Music by
RICHARD MARX

Moderately slow
G
C/G
G
C/G
mp
G
D/F♯
Em
Am
Em/G
When - ev - er I'm wea - ry from the bat - tles that rage in my
Some - times I just hold you, too caught up in me to
D/F♯
G
D/F♯
Em
head, you make sense of mad - ness when my
see I'm hold - ing a for - tune that
Am
Em/G
D/F♯
C
san - i - ty hangs by a thread. I lose my way,
heav - en has giv - en to me. I'll try to show

B7
Em
Em/D
C#m7♭5
4fr
but still you seem to un - der - stand. Now and for - ev -
you each and ev - 'ry way I can, now and for - ev -
Am7
Am7/D
D
1
G
C/G
- er, I will be your man.
- er, I will be your man.
2
G
C/G
B7
Now I can rest
Em
C
G
D
Em
C
my wor - ries and al - ways be sure that I won't be a - lone

G
D/F♯
Em
C
G
D
any - more.
If I'd on - ly known you were there all the time,
Am7
Cm(maj7)
8fr
Cm6
3fr
G
D/F♯
all this time.
Em
Am
Em/G
D/F♯
3
G
D/F♯
Em
Am
Em/G
3
D/F♯
C
B7
Un - til the day the o - cean does -

Em
Em/D
C♯m7♭5
4fr
Am7
- n't touch_ the sand,___ now and for - ev - er,___
C/D
D
G
C/G
I will be___ your man.___ Now and for - ev -
Am7
Am7/D
D
- er, I will be___ your
C
Cm6
3fr
G
C/G
D/G
G
man.
rit.

YOU AND I

Words and Music by
STEVIE WONDER

Slowly, with feeling
Fmaj7
B♭/F
B♭m/F
Fmaj7
B♭/F
Here we are on earth to - geth - er it's you and I.
I am glad at least in my life I found some - one
mf

B♭m/F
E7sus
A+
Dmaj7
God has made us fall in love, it's true. I've
that may not be here for - ev - er to see me through. But

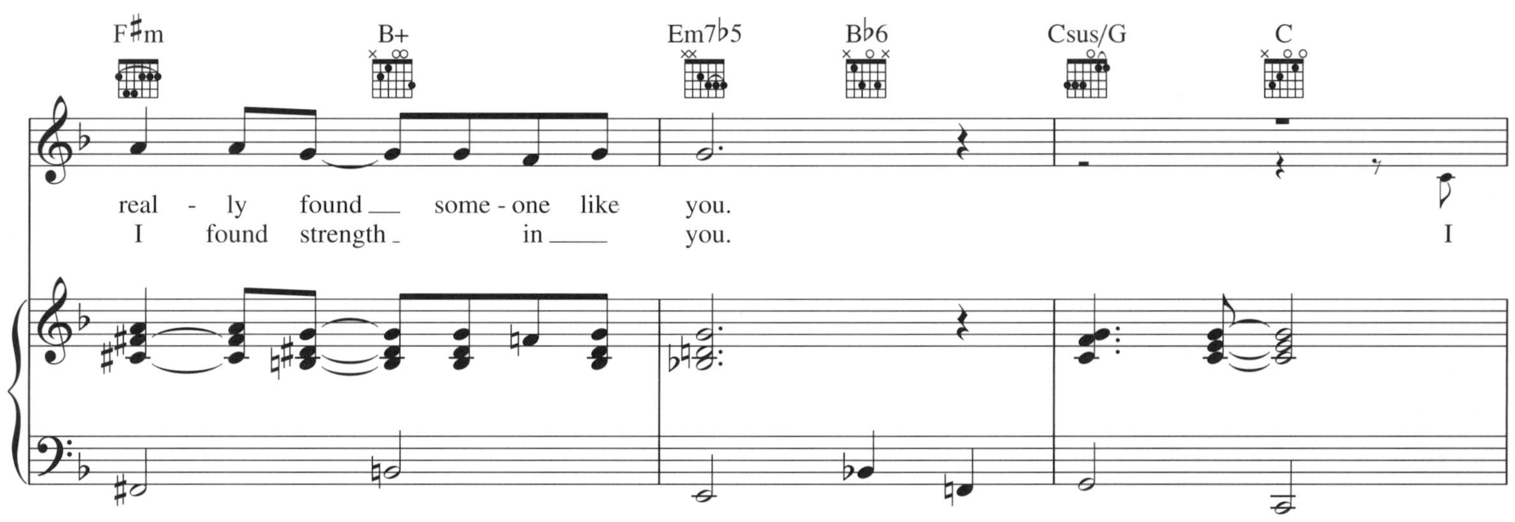
F♯m
B+
Em7♭5
B♭6
Csus/G
C
real - ly found some - one like you.
I found strength in you. I

Fmaj7
B♭/F
B♭m/F
Fmaj7
B♭/F
Will it stay, the love you feel for me? Will it say
on - ly pray that I have shown you a bright - er day,

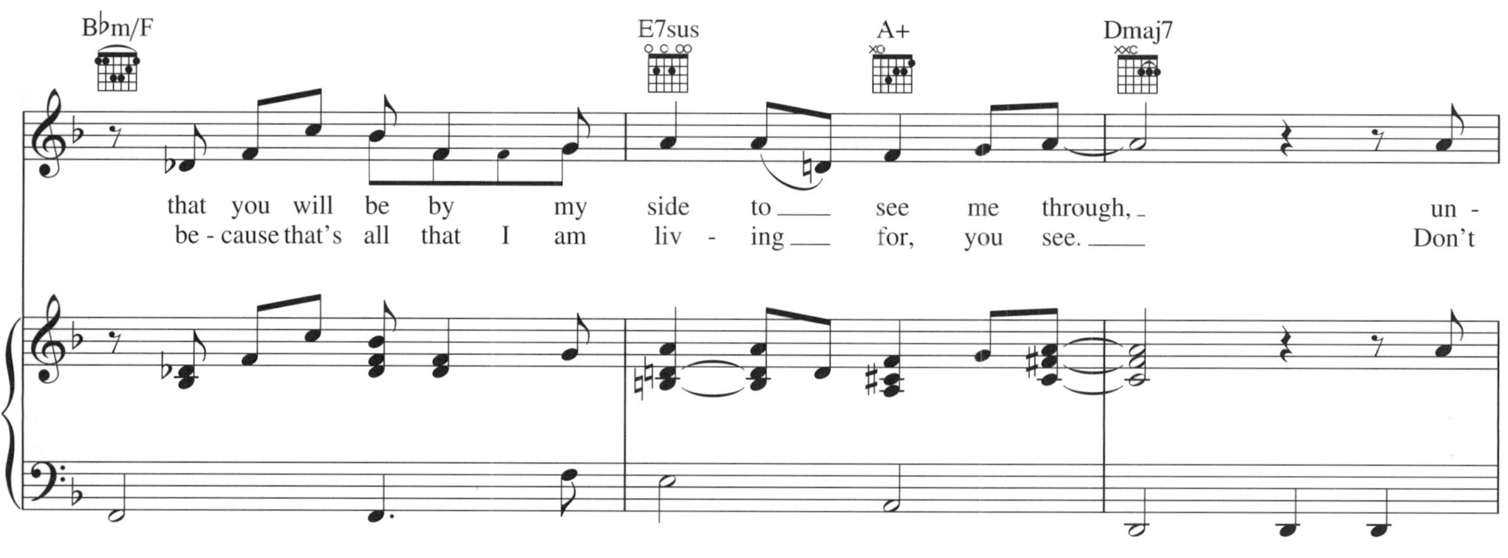
B♭m/F
E7sus
A+
Dmaj7
that you will be by my side to see me through, un -
be - cause that's all that I am liv - ing for, you see. Don't

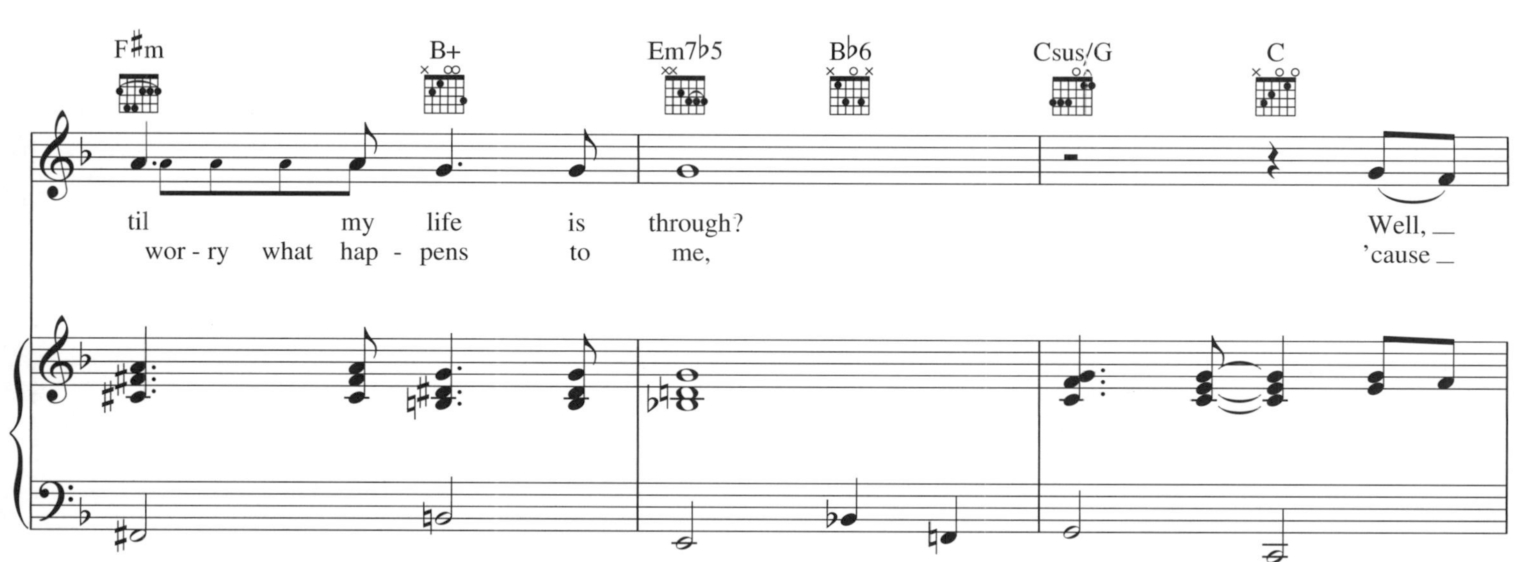
F♯m
B+
Em7♭5
B♭6
Csus/G
C
til my life is through? Well,
wor - ry what hap - pens to me, 'cause

Gm7
Bbm
F
in my mind — we can con - quer the world.
in my mind — you will stay here al - ways.
D7
G7
C7
In love, you and I. You and I. You and
In love, you and I. You and I. You and
1
F
Bb/F
Bbm/F
F
Bb/F
I.
Bbm/F
2
Fmaj7
I. —

YOU RAISE ME UP

Words and Music by BRENDAN GRAHAM
and ROLF LOVLAND

B♭sus2
F/A
B♭
F/A
C/G
still and wait here in the si - lence un - til you come and sit a while with
F5
Dm
B♭(add2)
3fr
F/A
C/E
me. You raise me up so I can stand on moun - tains; you raise me
mf
Dm
B♭(add2)
3fr
F/A
C
F
B♭(add2)/D
up to walk on storm - y seas. I am strong when I am on your
mp
F/C
B♭
F/C
C
F5
shoul - ders; you raise me up to more than I can be.

G C/G G Gmaj7/B C D
f
C/E C G/B C G/D D
3
G G/F♯ Em C G/B D/F♯
You raise me up so I can stand on moun - tains; you raise me
Em C G/B D G C/G
up to walk on storm - y seas. I am strong when I am on your
mp

G
C(add2)/G
G/D
D
G5
3fr
shoul - ders; you raise me up to more than I can be.
G7
C
F/C
C
There is no life, no life with - out its hun - ger; each rest - less
mf
C/E
F
G
F(add2)/A
F(add2)
heart beats so im - per - fect - ly. But when you come and I am filled with
C/G
F(add2)/A
C/G
G
C
G/B
won - der, some - times I think I glimpse e - ter - ni - ty. You raise me

Am F C/E G/B Am F
up so I can stand on moun - tains; you raise me up to walk on storm - y
f
C/E G C F C/G F(add2)/A
seas. And I am strong when I am on your shoul - ders. Oh, you raise me
3
C/G Am Fmaj7/A
very freely
up to more than I can be. You raise me
mf
p
very freely
N.C.
C G/C F/C Cmaj7(no3) F/C C
3fr
up to more than I can be.
8vb

GROW OLD WITH ME

Words and Music by
JOHN LENNON

Tenderly
mf
G D G G D/F♯ G Em Bm G D/F♯ G Em7 Bm7 C (add9) D
Grow old along with me. The best is yet to be. When our time has come, we will be as one.
along with me, two branch-es of one tree. Face the set-ting sun when the day is done.
along with me. What-ev-er fate de-crees, we will see it through, for our love is true.
God bless our

G
C (add9)
D
To Coda
1
G
love.
God bless our
love.
Grow old
2
G
Em
Bm
love.
Spend-ing our lives
to-geth-er,
Em
Bm
C
Am7
man and wife
to-geth-er.
World with-out end,
C/D
D
G
D/F♯
Em
world with-out end.

Am7
G/B
A/C♯
C (add9)
D
Em
Asus
A
C
D
G
C/G
G
D.S. al Coda
Grow old
CODA
C (add9)
D
G
Em7
Am7
D
love. God bless our love.
God bless our
G
D
D7
G
love.

Bless the Broken Road

Words and Music by MARCUS HUMMON,
BOBBY BOYD and JEFF HANNA

Moderately
C/E
Fsus2
G
Am
F
F/G
C/G
C
mf
I set out on a nar - row way many - y years a - go,
hop - ing I would find true love a - long the bro - ken road. But

Am7 G F C/E Dm7 G7sus
I got lost a time or two, wiped my brow and kept push-in' through.
C/E Fsus2 G Am F F/G C
I could-n't see how ev-er-y sign point-ed straight to you.
Dm C/E F6 C/F C Dm C/E G G7 C
But ev-er-y long lost dream led me to where you are.
3fr
Dm C/E F C/F Am7 G/B C Dm7 C
Oth-ers who broke my heart, they were like north-ern stars
3fr

G C Dm C/E F C/F C Dm C/E G G7 Am
3fr
pointing me on my way into your loving arms.
G/B C Dm7 C/E Fsus2 C/F
3fr
This much I know is true: that
3
C/E F G Am F F/G
To Coda
C/E Fsus2
God blessed the broken road that led me straight to you.
G Am F F/G C/G C C/E Fsus2
Yes, He did.

G Am7 F F/G C/G C C/E Fsus2
I think a - bout the years
G Am F G C C/E Fsus2
I've spent just pass- in' through. I'd like to have the time
G Am F F/G C Am11
3fr
I lost and give it back to you. But you just smile and take
G F C/E Dm7 F/G C/E Fsus2
my hand. You've been there, you un- der - stand it's all part of a grand-

D.S. al Coda
G
Am
F
F/G
C
Dm
C/E
- er plan
that is com - in' true.
Ev - er - y
CODA
N.C.
F/C
C
F(add9)
C
G
C
F
Am
Dm
C
G/B
C
F
F(add9)
C
Now I'm just a - roll - in' home

G
Am
G/B
C
into my lover's arms.
This much I
Dm7
C/E
Fsus2
C/F
3fr
C/E
Fsus2
know is true:
that God blessed the bro-
G
Am
F
F/G
C/E
Fsus2
ken road that led me straight to you,
G
Am
F
F/G
C/G
C
C/E
Fsus2
that God blessed the bro-

G
Am
F
G
- ken road
that led me straight
C/E
Fsus2
G
Am
to you.
F
F/G
C/G
C
C/E
Fsus2
G
Am
rit.
F
F/G
C

IT'S YOUR LOVE

Words and Music by
STEPHONY E. SMITH

Moderately
G
D
mf
C
D/C
C
D/C
C
G
Male: Danc-in' in the dark,
D/F♯
mid-dle of the night.
Em7
Tak-in' your heart
C
and hold-in' it tight.
G
E-mo-tion-al touch,

D/F♯
Em7
touch-in' my skin, and ask-in' you to do what
C
D
G
you've been do-in' all o-ver a-gain. Oh, it's a beau-ti-ful thing.
D
Em
C
Don't think I can keep it all in. I just got-ta let you know
D
G
what it is that won't let me go. Both: It's your love. It just does some-thin'

D
Em
to me. It sends a shock right through me. I can't get e-
C
G
nough. And if you won - der a - bout the spell I'm
D
C
D7/C
Cmaj9
un - der, Male: oh, Both: it's your love.
G
D/F#
Male: Bet - ter than I was, more than I am,

Em7
C
and all of this hap - pened
by tak - in' your hand.
G
D/F♯
And who I am now
is who I want - ed to be.
Em7
C
Both: And now that we're to - geth - er, I'm strong - er than ev - er. I'm hap - py and free.
D
G
D
Em
Oh, it's a beau - ti - ful thing. Don't think I can keep it all in.

C
D
Male: Oh, did you ask me why I've changed? All I got-ta do is say your sweet name.
Both: I just got-ta let you know what it is that won't let me go.
G
D
Both: It's your love. It just does some-thin' to me. It sends a shock right
Em
C
through me. I can't get e - nough. And if you
G
D
C
won - der a-bout the spell I'm un - der, Male: oh, Both: it's

D7/C
Cmaj9
To Coda
G
your love. Whoa.
D
Em
C
D.S. al Coda
Oh, it's a
CODA
C
D7/C
Cmaj9
It's your love.
C
D7/C
Cmaj9
G
It's your love.
rit.

Love Remains

Words and Music by TOM DOUGLAS
and JIM DADDARIO

G
D7
G
way.
Ma - ma smiles,
side.
Tears and sweat,
you.
We all live
G/B
Bm7
dad - dy cries,
mir - a -
they build a home
and raise a
and we all die,
but the
C
G
cle
be - fore their eyes.
fam - i - ly
of their own.
end
is not good - bye.
Bm/F♯
Em
Bm/D
They pro - tect us
till we're of
They share joy
and they share
The sun comes up
and sea - sons

C
Csus2
3fr
G
age.
pain.
change.
And through it all
D
To Coda
1
G
2
G
love re - mains.
Boy moves
Bm/F♯
Em
King - doms come and go, but they don't
Am7
D
last.
Be - fore you know, the fu -

G
Bm/F♯
- ture is the past.
In
Em
Am7
spite of what's been lost or what's been gained,
D
we are liv - ing proof that
G
G/B
C
love re - mains.

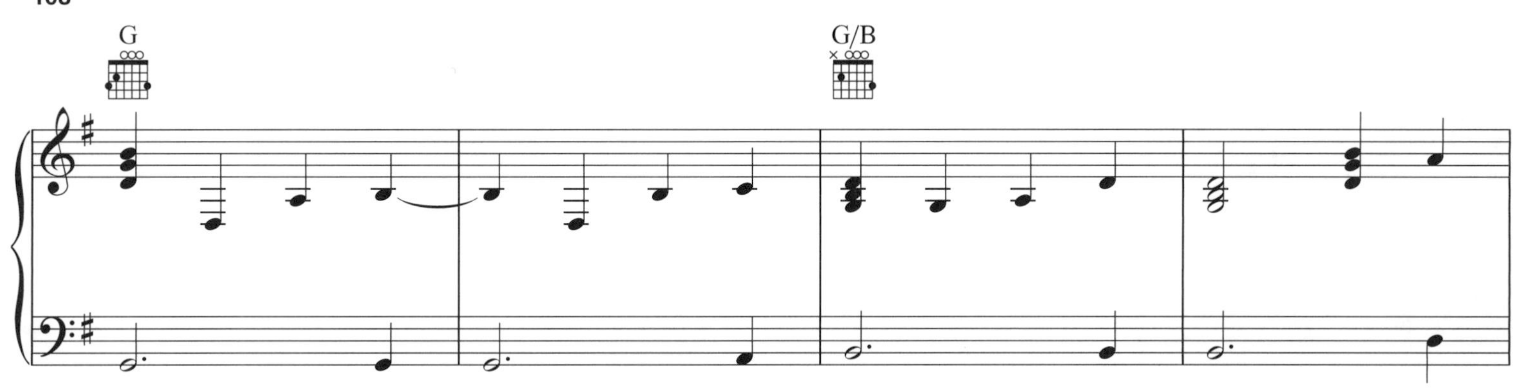
G
G/B

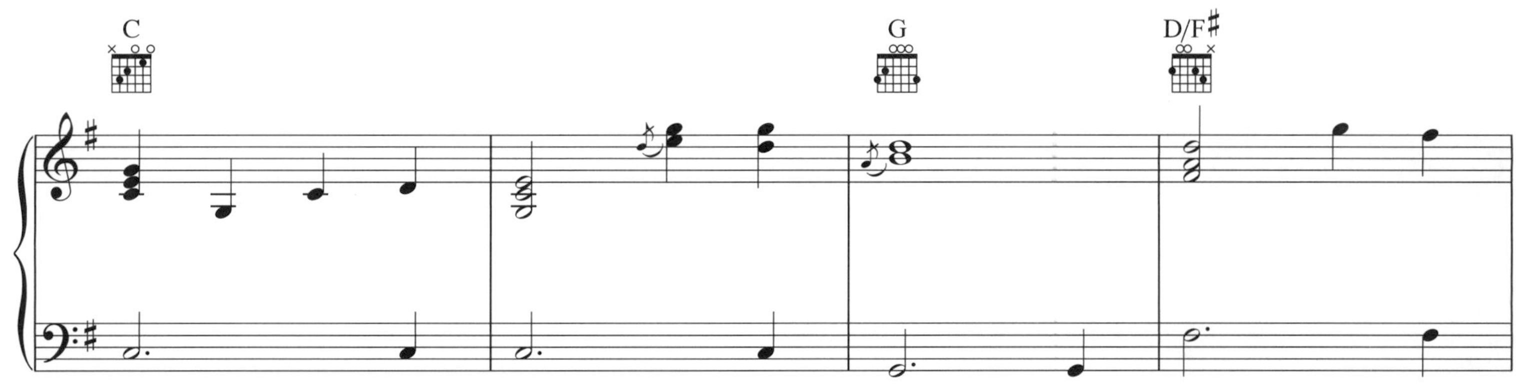
C
G
D/F♯

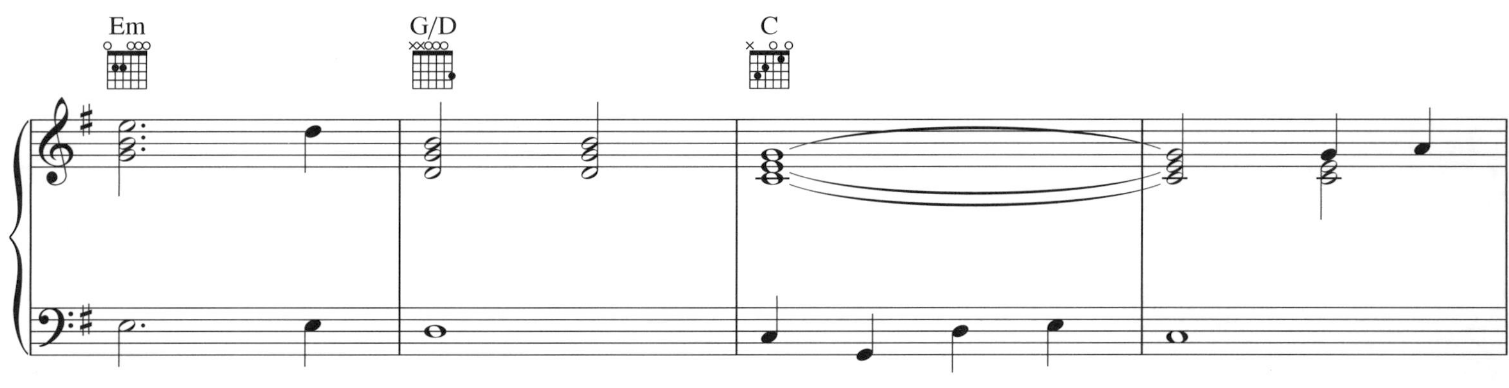
Em
G/D
C

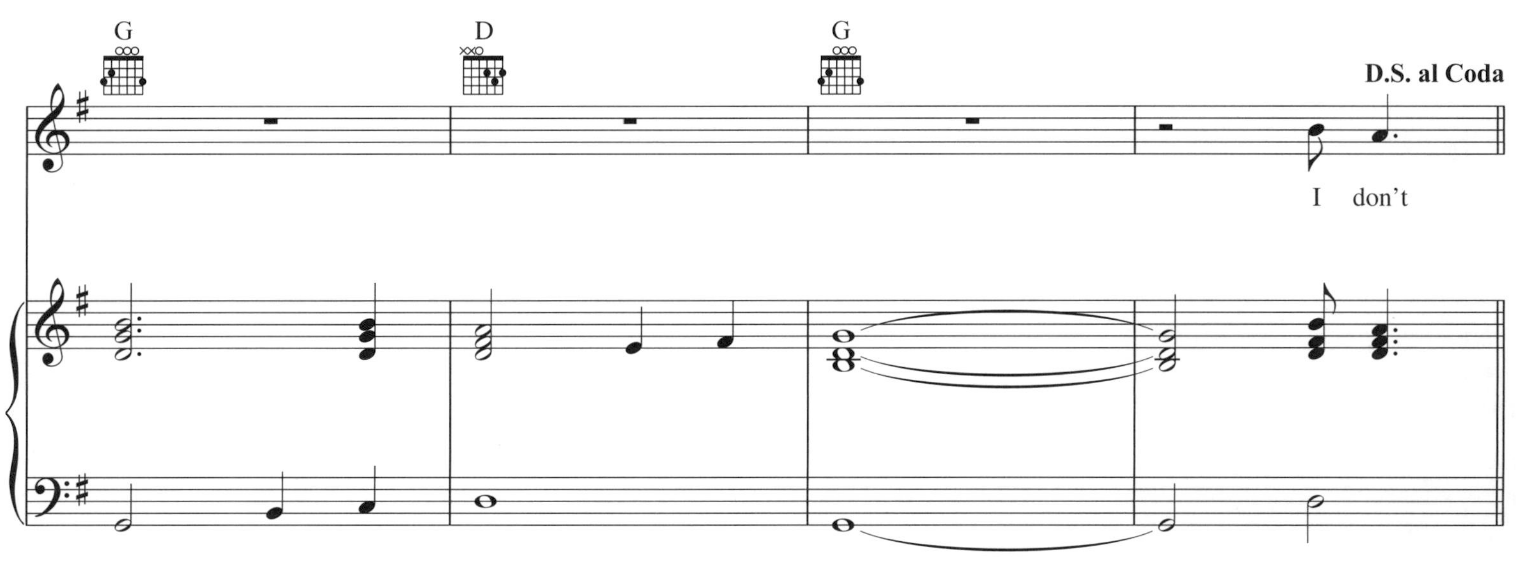
G
D
G
D.S. al Coda
I don't

CODA
G
Bm/F♯
Em
G/D
An e - ter - nal burn - ing
C
G
flame, hope lives on
D
C
G(add9)/B
and love re - mains.
Am7
D7sus
D7
G
rit.

Mama's Song

Words and Music by LUKE LAIRD,
KARA DioGUARDI, MARTI FREDERIKSEN
and CARRIE UNDERWOOD

G
A
Bm
now you have to let your ba - by fly.
A
G
A
You've giv - en me ev - 'ry - thing that I will
Bm7
A5
5fr
G
need to make it through this cra -
A
D
- zy thing called life.
And I know

Bm
F♯m/A
you watched me grow up and on-ly want what's best for
G
D/F♯
me. And I think I've found the an-swer to your
Em7
prayers.
D
And he is good,

Em7
G
so good.
He treats your lit - tle girl
D
A
like a real man should.
He is
D
Em7
good,
so
good.
G
D/F♯
He makes prom - is - es he keeps.
No, he's nev -

Em7
C
- er gon - na leave.
G
So, don't you wor - ry a - bout me.
A
Bm
A
Don't you wor - ry a - bout
G
A
Bm7
To Coda
me.

A
G
A
Ma - ma, there's no way you'll ev - er lose
Bm
A
G
me.
Giv - ing me a - way
A
Bm
A
is not good - bye.
G
A
Bm
As you watch me walk down to my fu - ture,

A
G
A
I hope tears of joy are in your
Em7
eyes.
D.S. al Coda
'Cause he is
CODA
D
G
And when I watch my ba - by grow
A
up, I'll on - ly want what's best for her. And I hope

Bm
G
she'll find the an - swer to my prayers.
Em7
D
And that she'll say he is good,
Em7
so good.
G
And he treats your lit - tle girl like a real man

D
Asus
A
D
should. He is good, so
Em7
G
good. He makes prom - is - es he keeps.
D/F#
Em7
C
No, he's nev - er gon - na leave.
So, don't you wor - ry a - bout

G
A
Bm
D
me.
Don't you wor - ry a - bout
Ma - ma, don't you wor - ry a -
bout me.
Don't you
Em7
wor - ry a - bout me.

Through the Years

Words and Music by STEVE DORFF
and MARTY PANZER

Cmaj7
D/C
Bm7
for an - y - one but you.
I lis - tened to be - fore.
D11
5fr
G
F#m7
B7
I swear we've been through ev - 'ry - thing there is.
I swear you've taught me ev - 'ry - thing I know.
Em7
Dm7
G7
Cmaj7
Can't i - mag - ine an - y - thing we've missed. Can't i - mag - ine
Can't i - mag - ine need - ing some - one so. But through the years it
G/B
Am7
D11
5fr
an - y - thing the two of us can't do. Through the
seems to me I need you more and more. Through the

G Em7 Am7

years, you've nev - er let me down, you've
years, through all the good and bad, I

D11 D/C Bm7 G/B Em7

turned my life a - round. The sweet - est days I've
knew how much we had. I've al - ways been so

Am7 D11 D/C Bm7

found I've found with you. Through the years, I've
glad to be with you. Through the years, it's

E7♭9 Am7 D7 D/C

nev - er been a - fraid, I've loved the life we've
bet - ter ev - 'ry day, you've kissed my tears a -

Bm7
E7♭9
Cmaj7
made. And I'm so glad I've stayed
way. As long as it's o - kay,
Bm7
Am7
D11
5fr
right here with you through the
I'll stay with you through the
1
G
Em7
F/C
C
years.
D11
5fr
2
G
I years.
3

E♭11
A♭
Through the years, when ev -
years, you've
Fm7
B♭m7
E♭11
E♭7/D♭
- 'ry - thing went wrong, to - geth - er we were
nev - er let me down, you turned my life a -
Cm7
F7
B♭m7
strong. I know that I be - longed right here with you.
round. The sweet - est days I've found I've found with you.
E♭11
E♭7/D♭
Cm7
F7♭9
Through the years, I nev - er had a
Through the years, it's bet - ter ev - 'ry

B♭m7
E♭7
E♭7/D♭
Cm7
3fr
doubt we'd al - ways work things out. I've
day, you've kissed my tears a - way. As
F7♭9
D♭
Cm7
3fr
learned what love's a - bout by lov - ing
long as it's o - kay, I'll stay with
B♭m7
E♭11
6fr
1
A♭
4fr
you through the years.
you through the
2
A♭
4fr
Through the years.

When You Say Nothing at All

Words and Music by DON SCHLITZ
and PAUL OVERSTREET

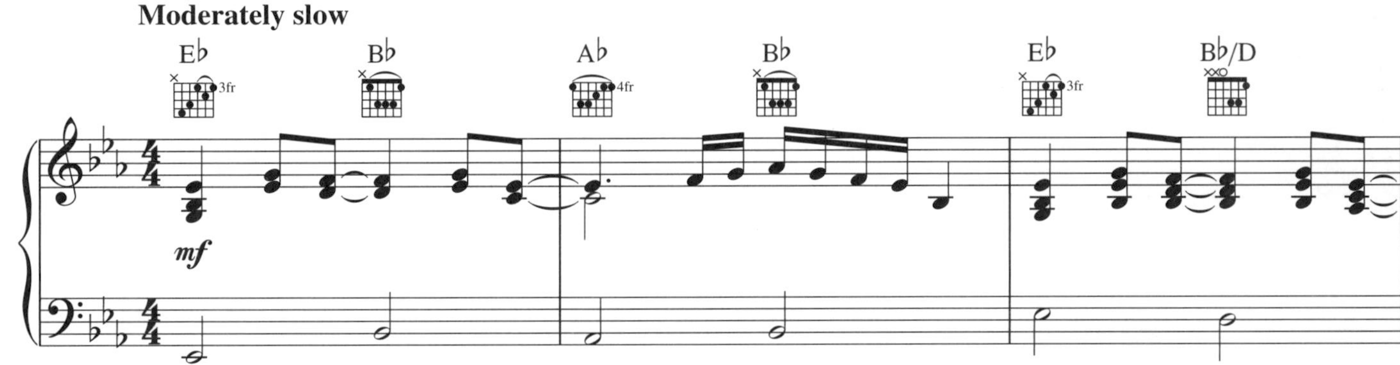
Moderately slow
E♭
3fr
B♭
A♭
4fr
B♭
E♭
3fr
B♭/D
mf

A♭/C
3fr
B♭
E♭
3fr
B♭
A♭
4fr
B♭
It's a - maz - ing how you can speak right to my heart.
All day long I can hear peo - ple talk - ing out loud,

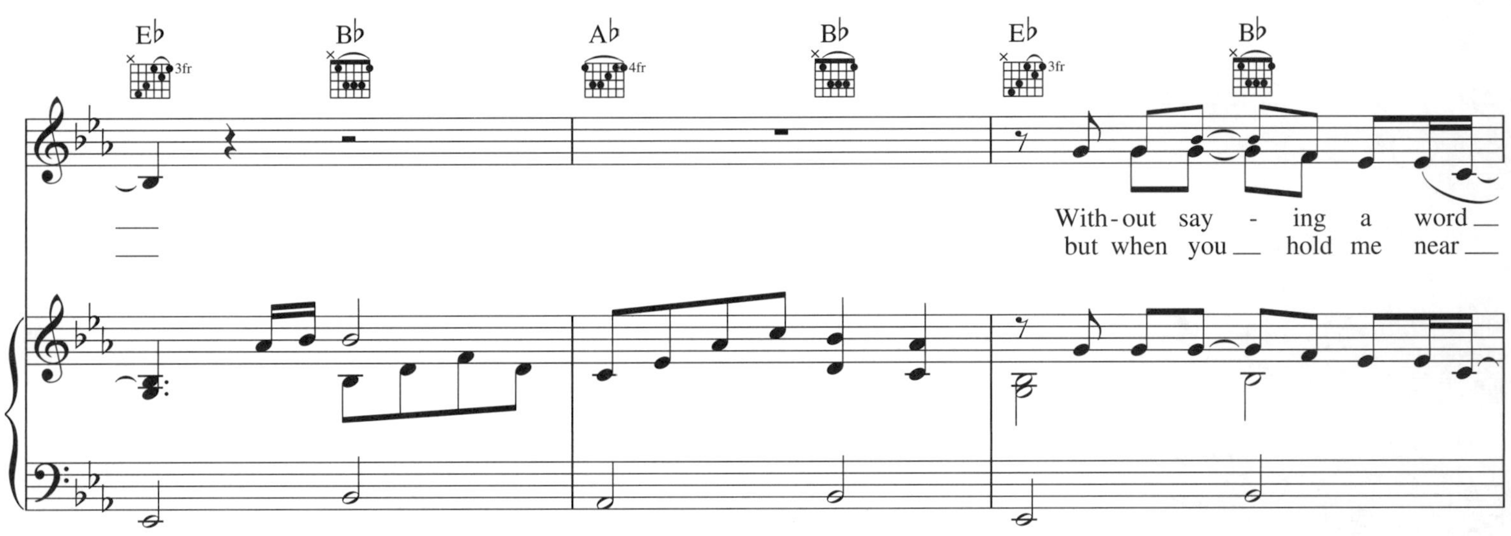
E♭
3fr
B♭
A♭
4fr
B♭
E♭
3fr
B♭
With - out say - ing a word
but when you hold me near

A♭
B♭
E♭
B♭
A♭
B♭
you can light up the dark.
you drown out the crowd.
Try as I may I could nev - er ex - plain
Old Mis - ter Web - ster could nev - er de - fine
what I hear when you don't say a thing.
what's be - ing said be - tween your heart and mine.
The
smile on your face lets me know that you need me. There's a

Eb
Bb
Ab
Bb
truth in your eyes say - ing you'll nev - er leave me. A
Eb
Bb
Ab
Bb
touch of your hand says you'll catch me if ev - er I fall.
Ab/C
Bb/D
Eb/G
Ab
To Coda
1
Bb
Now you say it best when you say noth-ing at all.
Eb
Bb
Ab
Bb
Eb
Bb/D

A♭/C
B♭
2
B♭
E♭
B♭
when you say noth - ing at all.
A♭
B♭
E♭
B♭
A♭
D.S. al Coda
The
CODA
B♭
E♭
B♭
A♭
B♭
when you say noth - ing at all.
E♭
B♭/D
A♭/C
B♭
E♭
rit.

Then

Words and Music by ASHLEY GORLEY,
BRAD PAISLEY and CHRIS DUBOIS

Moderately
Am7
Fsus2
Csus2
Gsus
3fr
mf
R.H.
C
G(add4)
F
I remember tryin' not to stare the night that I first met you.
I remember takin' you back to right where I first met you.
You had me mesmerized. And
You were so surprised. There were

Am7
F
C
G
three weeks lat - er in the front porch light, tak - in' for - ty - five min - utes to kiss good - night. I had - n't
peo - ple a - round, but I did - n't care. I got down on one knee right there, and
F
G/F
F5
G
told you yet, but I thought I loved you then.
once a - gain, I thought I loved you then.
C
G
And now you're my whole life,
But now you're my whole life,
now you're my whole
Am
G
F
G
world, and I just can't be - lieve the way I feel a - bout you, girl.

C
G
E/G♯
Like a riv - er meets the sea,
strong - er than it's ev - er been.
Am
G
F
We've come so far since that day,
and I thought I loved you
1
C
G
then.
2 C
G
then.

Am7
Fsus2
F(add♯4)
F(add9)
Guitar solo ad lib.
Solo ends
I can just
G
F
C
see you with a ba - by on the way, and I can just
G
F
C
see you when your hair is turn - in' gray. What I
Am
G/B
C
C/E
can't see is how I'm ev - er gon - na love you more.

F
But I've said that be - fore.
G
C
And now you're my whole
G
Am
G
life, now you're my whole world, and I just can't be - lieve
F
G
C
the way I feel a - bout you, girl. We'll look back some - day

G
E/G♯
Am
G
at this mo - ment that we're in,
and I'll look at you and
F
F(add♯4)
Fsus2
say,
"And I thought I loved you
C
Gsus
3fr
then,
and I thought I loved you
Am7
Fsus2
then."

C
Gsus
3fr
Ooh,
ooh,
Am7
Fsus2
ooh.
C
G
Ooh,
ooh,
Am7
Repeat and Fade
F
Optional Ending
F
ooh.

Angel

Words and Music by MARK HALL,
MATTHEW WEST and BERNIE HERMS

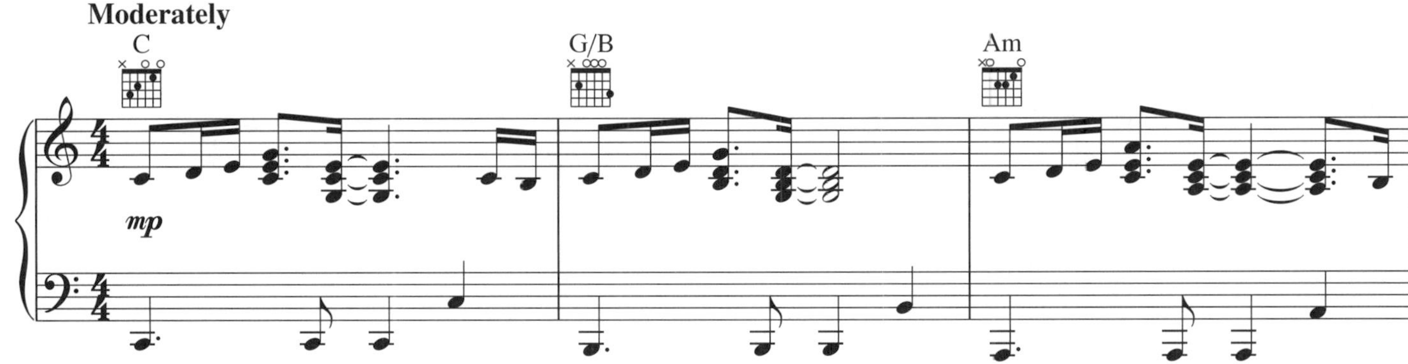
Moderately
C
G/B
Am
mp

Fmaj7
C
G/B
It was a day just like an - y oth - er day.

Am
Fmaj7
C
I was a boy just like ev - 'ry oth - er boy,
when a girl un - like an -

G/B
Am
- y I had seen, it's like she stepped out of a dream and
Fmaj7
Fsus2
in - to my world. It could-'ve been the sum - mer wind
G
F
play - ing with her hair. As the sun danced in her eyes,
G
F
we were stand - ing there. She smiled; I for - got my name,

G
C
'cause all I was think - ing:
May - be I'm cra - zy, but I'm pray -
mf
G
Am
F
- ing that an an - gel will love me, an an - gel will love me.
C
G
May - be I'm a fool, but I'm still fall - ing, ask - ing Heav - en a - bove
To Coda
Am
F
C
me for an an - gel to love me the rest of my life,

G/B
Am
Fmaj7
the rest of my life.
C
G/B
You're the proof that the Fa - ther an - swers prayer,
Am
Fmaj7
'cause some - how, some way,
you and I are stand - ing here
C
G/B
with a sa - cred prom - ise and a
ring that says it all. Oh, I've

Am
F
D.S. al Coda
just be - gun to fall, and from the deep - est part of me, I say, "I do."
CODA
F
me.
And af - ter all the chang - ing sea -
G
C/E
F
- sons have turned to years, the crowds are gone and the songs have fad -
G
C/E
F
- ed, well, I'll still be here, hold - ing you and thank - ing Heav -

G
C
-en for my an-gel.
May-be I'm cra-zy, but I'm pray-
mp
G
Am
-ing that an an-gel will love me, an an-gel will love
cresc.
F
C
G/B
me.
Well, may-be I'm cra-zy
for pray-ing an
mf
Am
F
C
an-gel will love me.
May-be I'm a fool, but I'm still fall-

G/B
Am
-ing, ask-ing Heav-en a-bove me for an an-gel to love
F
C
G/B
me the rest of my life, the rest of my life,
Am7/D
Fsus2
C
the rest of my life,
G/B
Am
Fsus2
the rest of my life.

God Gave Me You

Words and Music by
DAVE BARNES

C♯m
B7sus
F♯m7(add4)
and watch as the storm blows through. And I need you.
I'll be the flat-tered fool. But I need you.
Asus2
Bsus
Asus2
E
God gave me you for the ups and downs.
C♯m
Bsus
Asus2
E
God gave me you for the days of doubt.
C♯m
Bsus
Asus2
E
For when I think I've lost my way, there are no words

C♯m
Bsus
F♯m7(add4)
To Coda
here left to say. It's true:
1
Asus2
Bsus
Asus2
E5
God gave me you.
C♯m
B(add4)
Asus2
E5
C♯m
B(add4)
2
Asus2
Bsus
God gave me you.

C#m
4fr
Asus2
On my own, I'm on - ly
half of what I could be. I
E
B
can't do with - out you.
C#m
4fr
Asus2
We are stitched to - geth - er;
and what love has teth - ered, I
E
B
pray we nev - er un - do.
God

N.C.
gave me you for the ups and downs.
God
D.S. al Coda
gave me you for the days of doubt.
God
CODA
Asus2
Bsus
Asus2
E5
God gave me you,
C♯m
B(add4)
Asus2
E5
gave me you,

C♯m
4fr
B(add4)
Asus2
E5
gave _ me you.
C♯m
4fr
B(add4)
Asus2
E5
C♯m
4fr
B(add4)
Asus2
Repeat and Fade
Optional Ending
L.H.

HOLDING HANDS

Words and Music by STEVE GREEN,
GRANT CUNNINGHAM and MATT HUESMANN

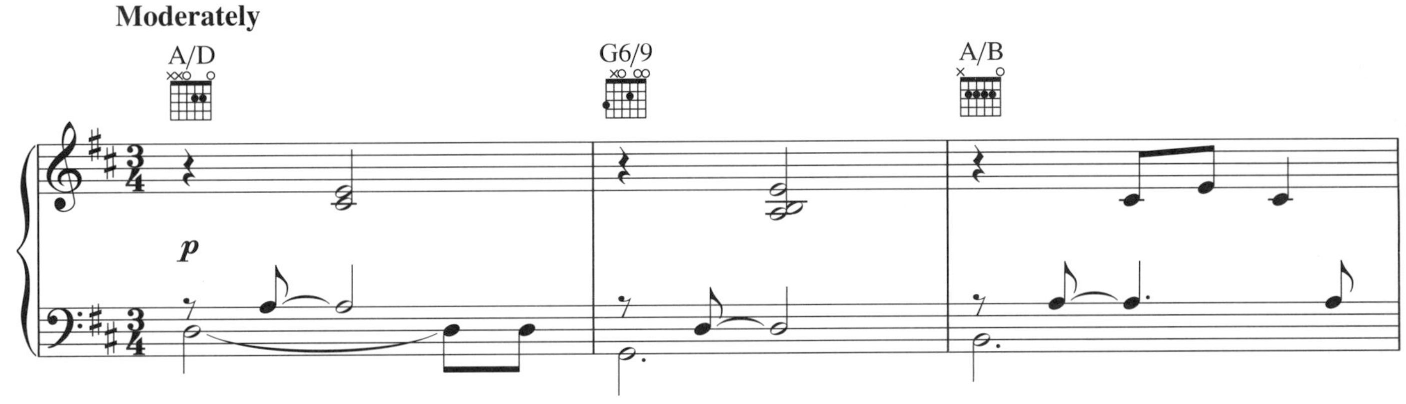
Moderately
A/D
G6/9
A/B
p

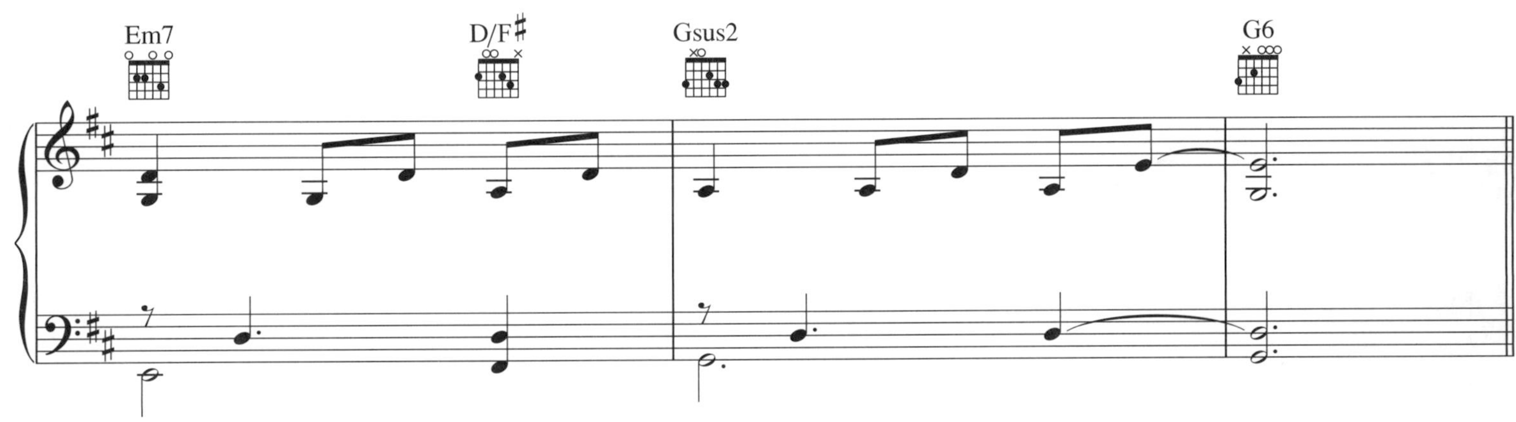
Em7
D/F♯
Gsus2
G6

D5
5fr
G(add2)
D/F♯
One day, far a - way, you gen - tly won my
Years fly; they hur - ry by. The sim - ple times are
Thoughts stray far a - way to all that lies a -

G(add2)
A/D
Bm7
heart, and one night by can - dle - light we
gone. Bills due; a kid or two. A
head; in frail days, when strength _ fades, will
Em7
Bm7/A
A
Asus
A
A♯dim
made a vow to nev - er part. And
week can feel eight days long. By
we still mean all that we said? Our
Bm7
F♯m7
Em7
then it seemed _ just like _ a dream _
fad - ing light _ let's kiss _ good - night, _
love's se - cure, _ so rest _ as - sured, _
Gsus2
D
Gsus2
_ when wide - eyed, side by side, we
_ and then we trace God's dai - ly grace,
_ come what may, 'til that day we'll

To Coda
Em7
A7sus
1
Dmaj9
4fr
faced the fu - ture hold - ing hands.
thank - ful we're still hold - ing hands.
walk for - ev - er hold -
Gmaj9
Bm11
Em11
5fr
2
D(add2)
Asus
There's a hope that won't
A
Dsus2
D
let go.
There's a
3

Asus
A
Bm7
truth we know; God is hold - ing us
Dmaj7/F♯
D/G
A/G
G
in His arms.
G(add2)
Em9
Bm7(♭6)
Gmaj13
3fr
A7sus
A
Em11
5fr
Bm7(♭6)
Gmaj13
3fr
Asus
A
D.S. al Coda

CODA
A7sus
Bm7(♭6)
D(add4)/C
3fr
- ing hands.
D
D/G
Em9
By God's grace, 'til that day we'll walk for - ev - er hold -
A
Asus
A
A7sus
A/D
G6/9
- ing hands.
Slower
Bm11
Em11
5fr
D

A Hundred More Years

Words and Music by BEN GLOVER
and FRANCESCA BATTISTELLI

* *Recorded a half step lower.*

C
D
wait - ed for love, and it was worth it. She wants to feel like this
mak - ing sure he's gon - na no - tice. He could watch her twirl
C
G
Em
D
for a hun - dred years. All this life still
for a hun - dred years. She'll grow up and
C
G/B
Am7
yet to live, and they can hard - ly wait. They can laugh,
she'll leave home, but un - til that day, they
G
D
they can cry. The fu -

G/B
C
- ture looks so beau - ti - ful and bright.
G
D
They can dance under the moon - light,
G/B
C
'cause God is smil - ing down on them to - night.
Em
D
C
And she he wants to stay right here,

G/B
Am7
1
Dsus
make it last
for a
hun - dred more years.
G5
3fr
2
Dsus
She's
hun - dred more years.
G
C
And it's on - ly time,
G/B
but it flies right by,
and to - day

Gm/B♭
D
is sweet - er than we know.
D6
D7
G
D
G/B

C
G
And so they dance
D
un - der the moon - light,
while God
G/B
is smil - ing down on them to - night.
C
Em
D
And they want to stay right here

C
G/B
Am7
for a
Dsus
G
hun - dred more years.
D
G/B
C
G5
3fr

I PROMISE
(WEDDING SONG)

Words and Music by CECE WINANS
and KEITH THOMAS

Dm
Gm
3fr
knew this heart of mine this
will and com - mit - ment to
til we're old and gray is the
E
Am
time would fall in love.
face an - y - thing.
vow to live as one.
1
C7
Mmm. All the
2, 3
C7
F
Dm
I will love you faith - ful - ly, for - ev - er un - con - di -

C
Gm
3fr
C
- tion - al - ly,
and my love I prom - ise.
F
Dm
Ev - 'ry - thing I have is yours,
you're ev - 'ry - thing I prayed
C
Gm
3fr
C
To Coda
and wait - ed for,
and my love I prom - ise
Dm
Gm
3fr
you.

C
F
C/E
D.S. al Coda
(take 2nd ending)
Now we be -
CODA
F
C/E
Dm
you.
Through the des - ert winds that blow, I'll
Am
C
walk you through the win - ters cold. I'll be there to keep the fire
G
Dm
a - live.
And when each pas - sage we en - dure, we

Am
E
Am
will stay strong, we can be sure our love survives.
C7
F
Dm
C
Gm
3fr
C
And my love I promise.
F
Dm
Ev - 'ry - thing I have is yours, you're ev - 'ry - thing I prayed

C
Gm
C
F
3fr
and wait - ed for, and my love I prom - ise, that I will love you faith - ful - ly,
Dm
C
Gm
for - ev - er un - con - di - tion - al - ly. And my love I
C
F
B♭/F
prom - ise you. Yeah, I prom -
Vocal ad lib. on repeats
Repeat ad lib. and Fade
Optional Ending
F
B♭/F
F
- ise you.

I WILL BE HERE

Words and Music by
STEVEN CURTIS CHAPMAN

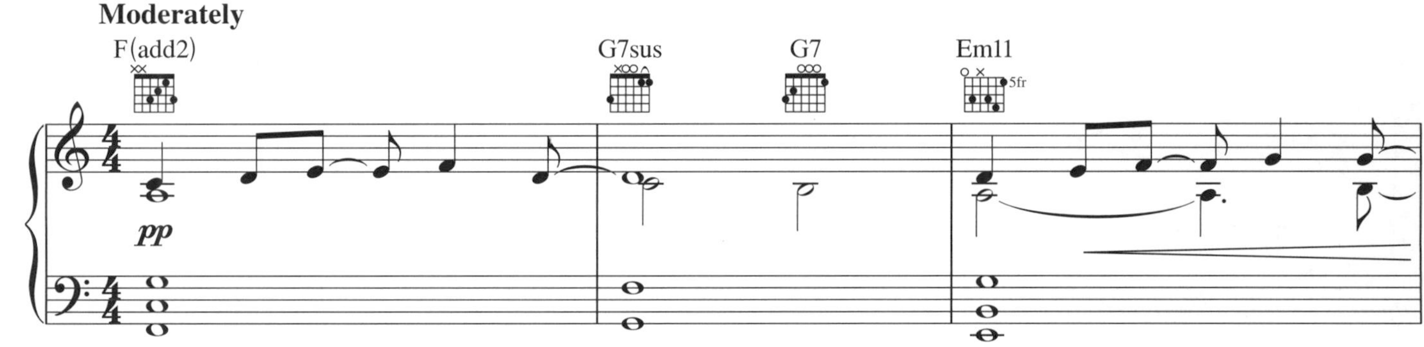
Moderately
F(add2)
G7sus
G7
Em11
5fr
pp

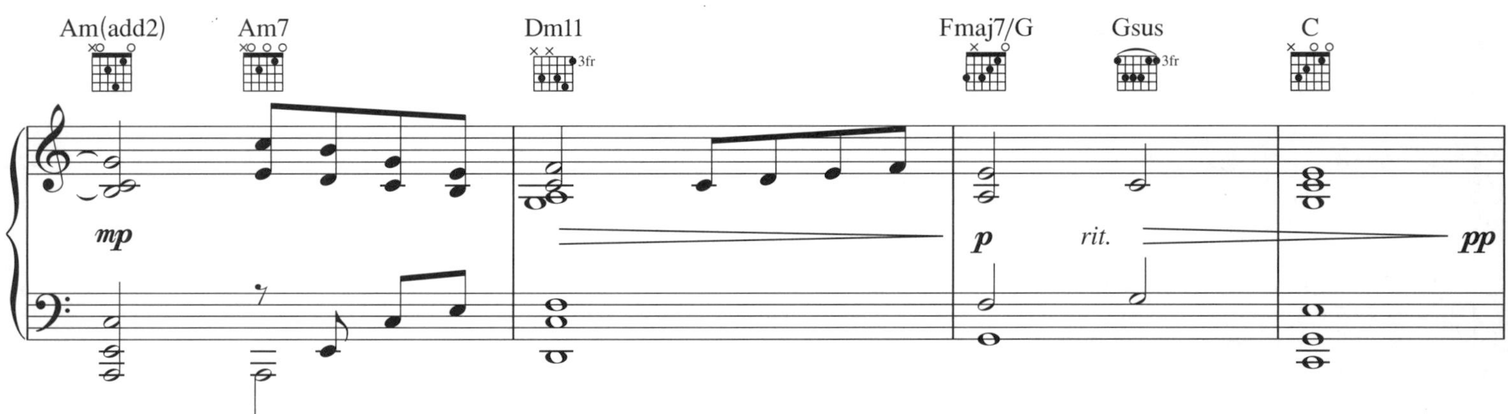
Am(add2)
Am7
Dm11
3fr
Fmaj7/G
Gsus
3fr
C
mp
p
rit.
pp

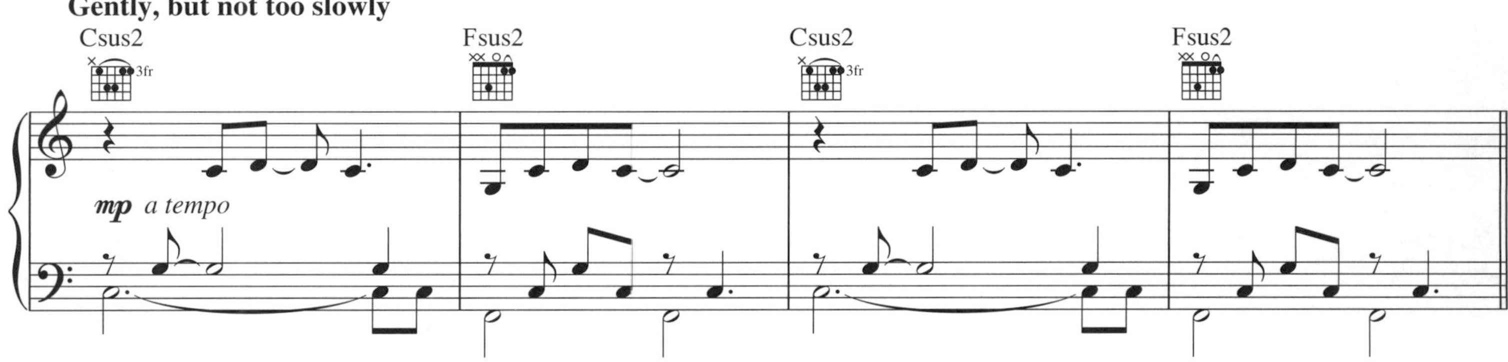
Gently, but not too slowly
Csus2
3fr
Fsus2
Csus2
3fr
Fsus2
mp a tempo

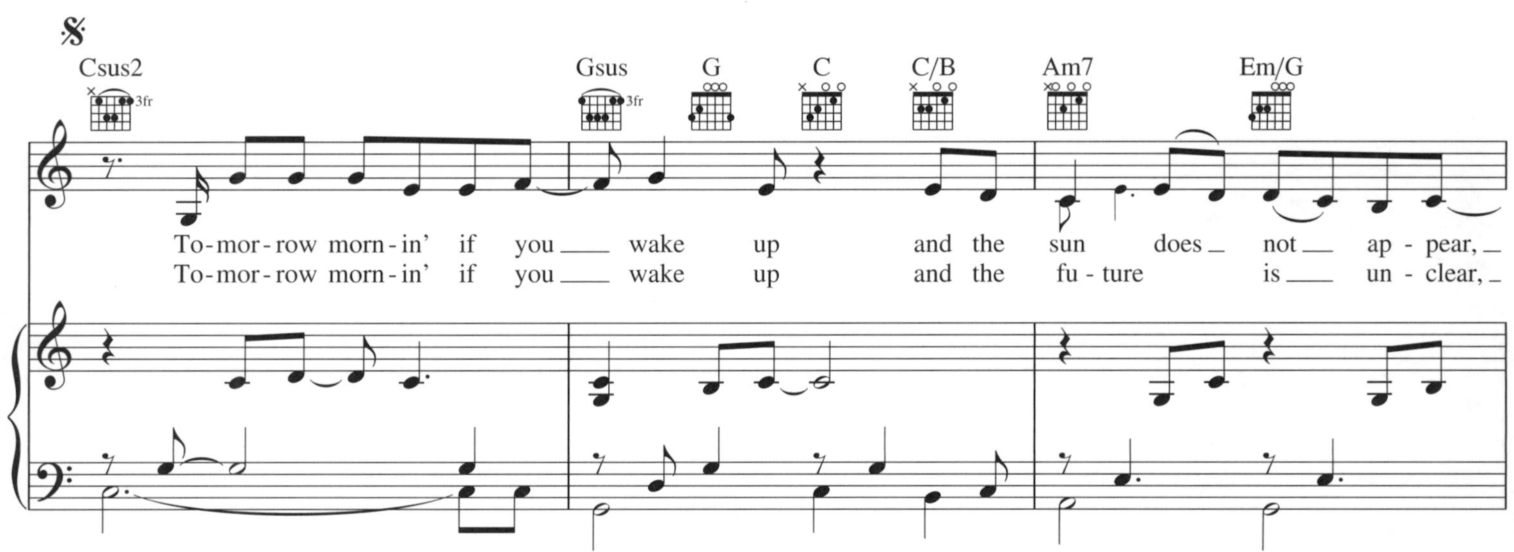
Csus2
3fr
Gsus
3fr
G
C
C/B
Am7
Em/G
To-mor-row morn-in' if you wake up and the sun does not ap - pear,
To-mor-row morn-in' if you wake up and the fu - ture is un - clear,

Fsus2
C/E
Dm7
G7sus
G7
I, I will be here.
I, I will be here.
Csus2
Fsus2
Csus2
If in the dark we lose sight
As sure as sea - sons are made
Gsus
G
C
C/B
Am7
Em/G
Fsus2
C/E
of love, hold my hand and have no fear, 'cause
for change, our life-times are made for years, so
Dm7
G7sus
G7
Csus2
I, I will be here.
I, I will be here.

C
G/B
Am
Am7/G
5fr
C/D
D7
I will be here when you feel like be - in' qui -
I will be here and you can cry on my shoul -
mf
G
Gmaj7/F♯
Cmaj7/E
F
C/E
- et. When you need to speak your mind, I will lis -
- der. When the mir - ror tells us we're old - er, I will hold
Dm7
E+
E7
Am
Am7/G
5fr
C/D
D7
- ten. And I will be here when the laugh-ter turns to cry -
you. And I will be here to watch you grow in beau -
3
G
G7/F
Cmaj7/E
F
C/E
- in', through the win-nin', los - in' and try - in'. We'll be to-geth -
- ty and tell you all the things you are to me. I will be here.

To Coda
Dm7
Dm7/G
Csus2
3fr
- er,
'cause I will be here.
decresc.
Fsus2
Csus2
3fr
Fsus2
D.S. al Coda
CODA
Dm7/G
E7/G#
Am
C/D
D7
Hmm,
I will be true to the prom-
G7
G7/F
C(add2)/E
F
C/E
- ise I have made to you and to the One

Dm7
Dm7/G
G7
Dm7
G7sus
G7
who gave you to me.
C
Csus
G
C
G/B
Am
Em/G
Fsus2
C/E
Dm7
G7sus
G7
Csus2
I, I will be here.
Fsus2
Csus2
Gsus
G
C
C/B
And just as sure as sea-sons are made for change, our

Am7
Em/G
Fsus2
C/E
Dm7
life-times are made for years, so I,
Dm7/G
G7
G♯dim7
Am
Am7/G
5fr
Dm7
I will be here. We'll be to-geth-er.
Dm7/G
G
C
I will be here.
F(add2)
C/E
Dm7
Dm7/G
C

IF YOU COULD SEE WHAT I SEE

Words and Music by GEOFF MOORE
and STEVEN CURTIS CHAPMAN

D♭
E♭sus
E♭
E♭7/G
A♭
Now I can't be - lieve you're stand - ing here.
won - der - ing what I see in you.
E♭/G
A♭
E♭/G
If beau - ty is all in the eye
It's all of the light and the grace;
Fm
Cm/E♭
D♭
of the be - hold - er, then I wish you could see
your be - lief in me drives me to say that I prom - ise you
B♭/D
D♭/E♭
A♭
the love for you that lives in me.
a faith - ful love, for - ev - er true.
And you would know

Fm7
Db
Eb
3fr
you have my heart,
if you could see
what I see;
Ab
4fr
Fm7
Db
that a treas - ure's what you are,
if you could see
Eb/G
3fr
Fm
Eb/G
3fr
what I see;
cre - at - ed to be
the on -
the on -
Db
Ab/C
Eb/Bb
6fr
Ab
4fr
Db
Ab/C
Bbm7
- ly one for me,
- ly one for me.
if you could see
If you could see,

1
E♭/G
A♭
Fm
what I see.
D♭maj7
D♭/E♭
E♭7
D♭/E♭
2
E♭/G
D♭(add9)
then you'd un - der - stand
A♭/C
why I fall down to my knees; and I pray
Fm7
Cm7
Fm7
B♭m7
A♭/C
my love will be wor - thy of the One who gave His life

D♭6
E♭
3fr
A♭
4fr
Fm7
so our love could be.
D♭maj7
D♭/E♭
E♭
3fr
A♭
4fr
If you could see what I see,
Fm7
D♭maj7
D♭/E♭
E♭
3fr
Fm
if you could see what I see;
E♭/G
3fr
D♭
A♭/C
B♭m7
A♭
4fr
D♭
you're cre - at - ed to be the per - fect one for

A♭/C
B♭m7
E♭/G
me, if you could see what I
A♭
Fm
D♭
D♭/E♭
E♭
D♭/E♭
see.
A♭
E♭/G
Fm
If beau-ty is all in the eye of
A♭/E♭
D♭maj7
D♭/E♭
E♭7
A♭(add2)
the be-hold - er, then I am be-hold - ing true beau-ty.

Love Never Fails

Words and Music by BRANDON HEATH
and CHAD CATES

A♭ D♭/A♭ Fm D♭ A♭ E♭/G

love does not hide, love does not keep locked in - side.
love al - ways hopes, love still be - lieves when you don't.

D♭/F E♭/G A♭ D♭

Love is the riv - er that flows through, and
Love is the arms that are hold - ing you,

D♭ E♭

love nev - er fails
love nev - er fails

1

A♭ D♭/A♭ A♭ D♭/A♭

you.

2

D♭ E♭ D♭ E♭

you.

D♭
E♭
D♭
E♭
3fr
When my heart_ won't make a sound,
D♭
E♭
Fm
when I can't_ turn back a - round,
when the sky_ is_ fall - ing down,_
E♭/G
A♭
D♭
4fr
_ noth - ing is_ great - er than this,_ great - er than this._
A♭
D♭/A♭
'Cause love is right here, love is a - live,

Fm Db Ab Eb/G Db/F Eb/G
love is the way, the truth, the life.
Love is the riv - er that
Ab Db Db/F Eb/G Ab Db
flows through, love is the arms that are hold - ing you, and
Db/F Eb/G Ab Db Eb
love is the place you will fly to. Love nev - er fails
Ab Db/Ab Ab Db/Ab Ab
you.
4fr
3fr

THE GIFT OF LOVE

Words by HAL H. HOPSON
English Melody adapted by HAL H. HOPSON

Moderately
G(add2)
C6/G
Am
mp
G
Am7
Though I may speak with brav - est
G
Em
fire, and have the gift
Am7
D
to all in - spire, and have not

G
C
Am7
G
love; my words are vain,
mf
Am7
Dsus
D
C
as sound - ing brass and hope - less
rall.
G
Em7
C
gain.
mp a tempo
D
G
Though I may give

Am7
G
Bm
Em
all I pos - sess,
and striv - ing so
Am7
D
Am7
G6/9
my love pro - fess,
but not be giv'n
Am11
3fr
G
Am7
D
by love with - in,
the prof - it soon
C
G(add2)
C6/G
Am
turns strange - ly thin.
rall.
p a tempo

G
Am7
Come, Spir - it, come, our hearts con -
mf
G
Em
trol. Our spir - its long
Am7
D
to be made whole. Let in - ward
cresc.
G
Am7
G
love guide ev - 'ry deed.
f

Am7
D
C
By this, we wor - ship and are
rall.
G(add2)
D/F#
freed. A - men, A -
mf a tempo
Em
Am
G
Dsus
D
G
men, A - men, A - men.
rit.
mp a tempo
Em7
C
G
rit.

gratefully dedicated to my friend John Charles Thomas

THE LORD'S PRAYER

By ALBERT HAY MALOTTE

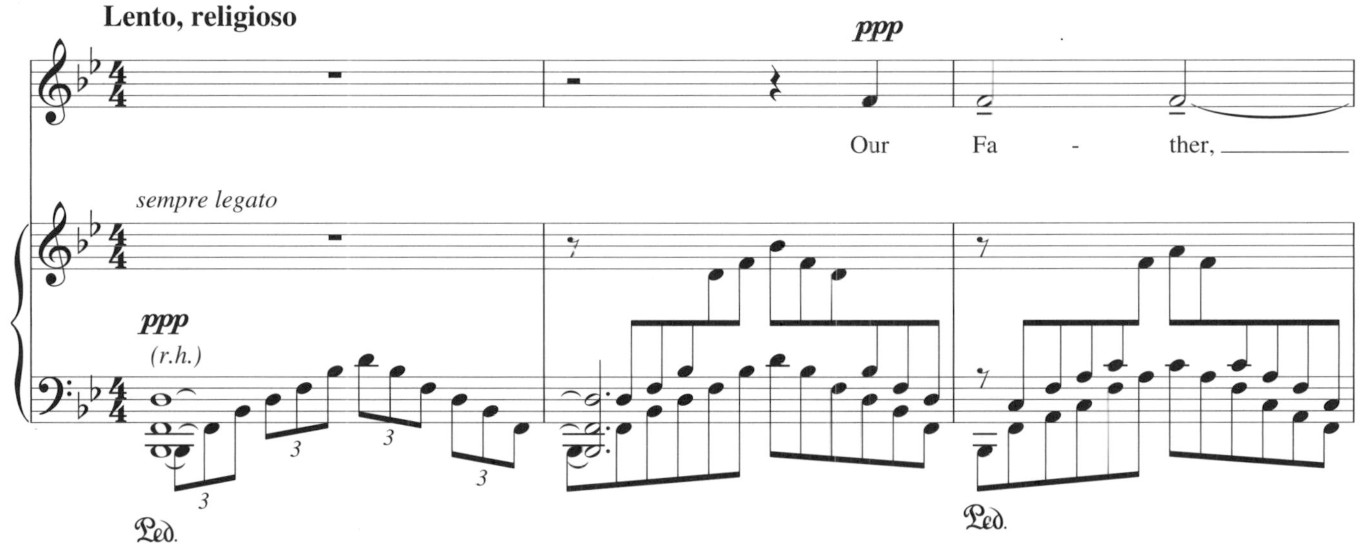

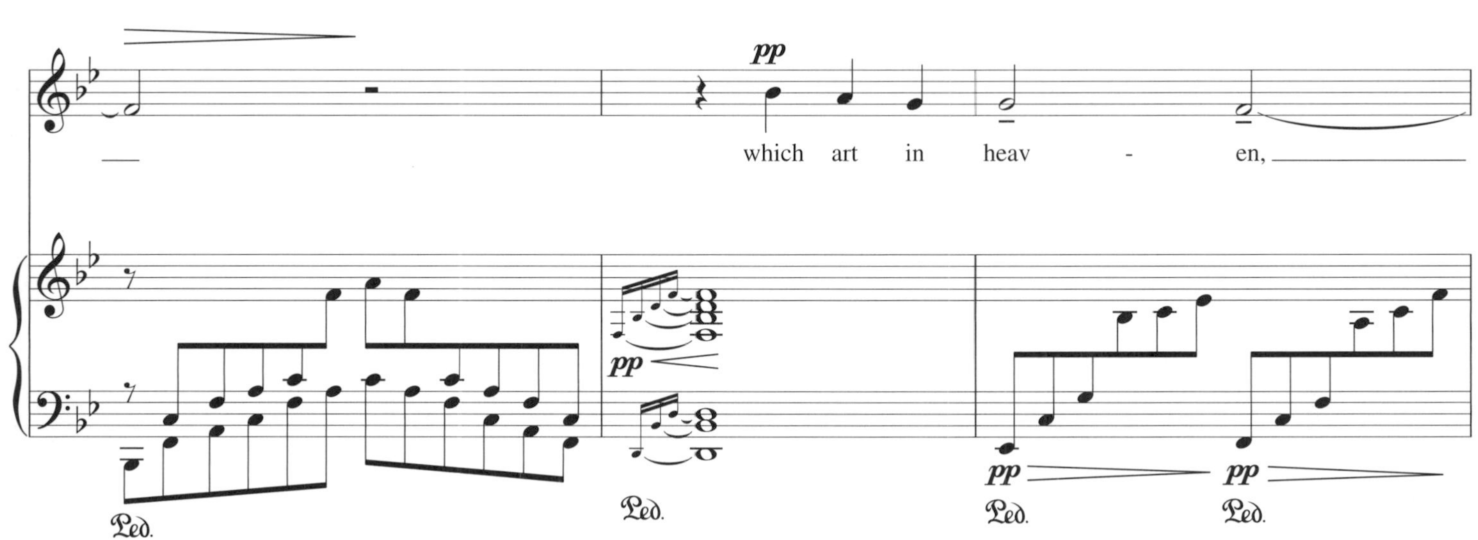

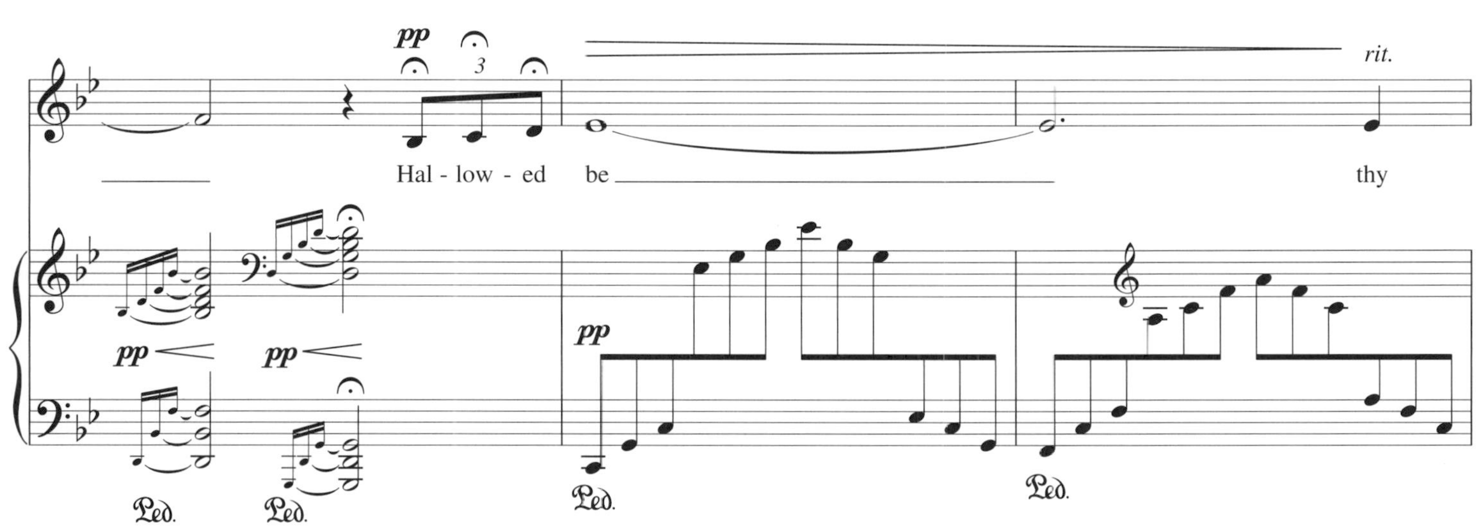

a tempo
accel.
poco più mosso
p
Name.
Thy king - dom
pp
p
Ped.
come.
Thy will be done in
mp
p
mp
poco cresc.
p
earth, As it is in heav - en.
Tempo I
p
pp

L'istesso tempo
p
pp molto espressivo e sempre legato
pp
Give us this day our
r.h.
pp
p
poco accel.
p
p
dai - ly bread. And for-give us our debts, As
tres - pass-es As
r.h.
l.h.
Ped.

rallentando
a tempo
we for - give our debt - ors.
we for-give those who tres-pass a - gainst us.
pp
p
Ped.
p
mf
And lead us not in - to temp - ta - tion; But de - liv - er us from
mp
rit.
Poco meno mosso, e sonoramente
f
e - vil: For thine is the king - dom, and the

ten.
ff
pow - er, and the glo - ry, for -
ten.
ff
ten.
Ped.
Ped.
opt.
f
ev - er.
ev - er and ev - er. A -
f
Ped.
Ped.
Ped.
Tempo I
rallentando e morendo
mf
p
men.
men.
mf
p
pp
ppp
Ped.
Ped.

GREAT IS THY FAITHFULNESS

Words by THOMAS O. CHISHOLM
Music by WILLIAM M. RUNYAN

A7
D
Em
D/F♯
Thou chang - est not, Thy com - pas - sions they
Join with all na - ture in man - i - fold
Strength for to - day and bright hope for to -
G
G♯dim7
D/A
fail not; As Thou hast been Thou for -
wit - ness To Thy great faith - ful - ness,
mor - row, Bless - ings all mine, with ten
A7
D
A
A/C♯
ev - er wilt be.
mer - cy and love.
thou - sand be - side!
Great is Thy
G/D
D
B
B/D♯
4fr
Am/E
Em
faith - ful - ness! Great is Thy faith - ful - ness!

A7
D
Dm6
A/E
E7
Morn - ing by morn - ing new mer - cies I
A
A7
D
see. All I have need - ed Thy
Em
D/F♯
G
G♯dim7
hand hath pro - vid - ed; Great is Thy
D/A
Em7
A7
1, 2
D
3
D
faith - ful - ness, Lord, un - to me! me!
8vb

WEDDING SONG
(THERE IS LOVE)

Guitar: Capo I

Words and Music by
PAUL STOOKEY

(D5) (A/C♯)
E♭5 B♭/D

now to be a - mong you at the call - ing of your hearts.

(G(add2)/D)
A♭(add2)/E♭

Rest as - sured, this trou - ba - dour is

(D5)
E♭5

act - ing on His part. The

𝄋 (D5) (A/C♯) (G(add2)/D)
E♭5 B♭/D A♭(add2)/E♭

un - ion of } your spir - its here has caused Him to re - main,
mar - riage of }

(D5)
E♭5
(Bm)
Cm
(Bm/C♯)
Cm/D
(D5)
E♭5
for when - ev - er two or more of you are
(A/C♯)
B♭/D
(G(add2)/D)
A♭(add2)/E♭
gath-ered in His name there is love,
there is
ah, there's
(D5)
E♭5
(Dsus)
E♭sus
(D)
E♭
(E)
F
love.

To Coda
(Esus2)
(E7(add4))
5fr
(G)
(Gmaj7)
(G6)
(G)
Fsus2
F7(add4)
A♭
A♭maj7
A♭6
A♭
(D)
(Dsus)
(D)
(Dsus)
(D5)
E♭
E♭sus
E♭
E♭sus
E♭5
Well, a man shall leave his
(A/C♯)
(G(add2)/D)
(D5)
B♭/D
A♭(add2)/E♭
E♭5
moth - er, and a wom - an leave her home, and
(Bm)
(Bm/C♯)
(D5)
(A/C♯)
Cm
Cm/D
E♭5
B♭/D
they shall trav - el on to where the two shall be as

(D5)
(A/C♯)
E♭5
B♭/D
3
one. As it was in the be - gin - ning, is
(G(add2)/D)
(D5)
(Bm)
(Bm/C♯)
A♭(add2)/E♭
E♭5
Cm
Cm/D
now un - til the end. Wom - an draws her life
(D5)
(A/C♯)
E♭5
B♭/D
from man and gives it back a - gain, and there is
(G(add2)/D)
A♭(add2)/E♭
love,

(D5)
Eb5
there is love.
(Dsus)
Ebsus
(D)
Eb
(E)
F
(Esus2)
Fsus2
(E7(add4))
5fr
F7(add4)
(G)
Ab
(Gmaj7)
Abmaj7
(G6)
Ab6
(G)
Ab
(D)
Eb
(Dsus)
Ebsus
(D)
Eb
(Dsus)
Ebsus
Well then,
(G)
Ab
(G/F♯)
Ab/G
(Em7)
Fm7
(G/D)
Ab/Eb
(A/C♯)
Bb/D
what's to be the rea - son for be - com-ing man and wife?

(D)
(Dsus)
(G)
(G/F♯)
(Em7)
(G/D)
E♭
E♭sus
A♭
A♭/G
Fm7
A♭/E♭
Is it love that brings you here, or
(A/C♯)
(D)
(Dsus)
(D5)
B♭/D
E♭
E♭sus
E♭5
love that brings you life? For if lov - ing is the an -
(A/C♯)
(G(add2)/D)
(D5)
B♭/D
A♭(add2)/E♭
E♭5
- swer, then who's the giv - ing for? Do
(Bm)
(Bm/C♯)
(D5)
(A/C♯)
Cm
Cm/D
E♭5
B♭/D
you be - lieve in some - thing that you've nev - er seen be -

(G(add2)/D)
A♭(add2)/E♭
fore? Oh, there's love,
oh, there's love.
(D5)
E♭5
(Dsus)
E♭sus
(D)
E♭
(E)
F
(Esus2)
Fsus2
(E7(add4))
F7(add4)
5fr
(G)
A♭
(Gmaj7)
A♭maj7
(G6)
A♭6
(G)
A♭
(D)
E♭
(Dsus)
E♭sus

(D)
E♭
(Dsus)
E♭sus
(D5)
E♭5
(Dsus)
E♭sus
(D)
E♭
(A/C♯)
B♭/D
(Bm)
Cm
(Bm/C♯)
Cm/D
(D5)
E♭5
(A/C♯)
B♭/D
D.S. al Coda
Oh, the
CODA
(G6)
A♭6
(G)
A♭
(D)
E♭
(Dsus)
E♭sus
(D)
E♭

O Perfect Love

Words by DOROTHY FRANCES GURNEY
Music by JOSEPH BARNBY

B♭7/F
E♭/G
A♭
be the love which knows no end - ing,
hope and qui - et, brave en - dur - ance,
day the glo - rious un - known mor - row
1, 2
B♭
B♭7/A♭
E♭/G
A♭6
Fm
B♭7
Whom Thou for - ev - er - more dost join in
With child - like trust that fears no pain nor
E♭
B♭7
one.
death.
3
Fm7
B♭
Bdim7
Cm
A♭6
That dawns up - on e - ter - nal
Fm7
B♭7
E♭
A♭
E♭
love and life.

The Most Romantic Music In The World

Arranged for piano, voice, and guitar

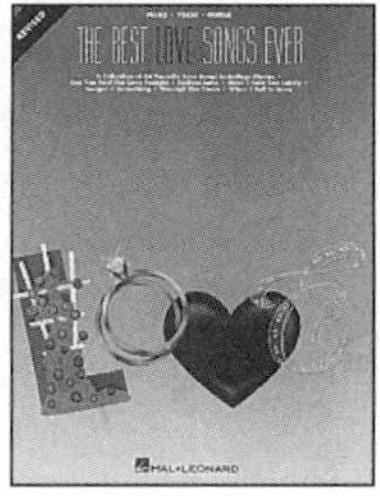

The Best Love Songs Ever – 2nd Edition

This revised edition includes 65 romantic favorites: Always • Beautiful in My Eyes • Can You Feel the Love Tonight • Endless Love • Have I Told You Lately • Misty • Something • Through the Years • Truly • When I Fall in Love • and more.

00359198 ....$19.95

The Big Book of Love Songs – 2nd Edition

80 romantic hits in many musical styles: Always on My Mind • Cherish • Fields of Gold • I Honestly Love You • I'll Be There • Isn't It Romantic? • Lady • My Heart Will Go On • Save the Best for Last • Truly • Wonderful Tonight • and more.

00310784 ....$19.95

The Christian Wedding Songbook

37 songs of love and commitment, including: Bonded Together • Cherish the Treasure • Flesh of My Flesh • Go There with You • Household of Faith • How Beautiful • I Will Be Here • Love Will Be Our Home • Make Us One • Parent's Prayer • This Is the Day • This Very Day • and more.

00310681 ....$16.95

The Bride's Guide to Wedding Music

This great guide is a complete resource for planning wedding music. It includes a thorough article on choosing music for a wedding ceremony, and 65 songs in many different styles to satisfy lots of different tastes. The songs are grouped by categories, including preludes, processionals, recessionals, traditional sacred songs, popular songs, country songs, contemporary Christian songs, Broadway numbers, and new age piano music.

00310615 ....$19.95

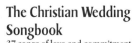

Broadway Love Songs

50 romantic favorites from shows such as *Phantom of the Opera, Guys and Dolls, Oklahoma!, South Pacific, Fiddler on the Roof* and more. Songs include: All I Ask of You • Bewitched • I've Grown Accustomed to Her Face • Love Changes Everything • So in Love • Sunrise, Sunset • Unexpected Song • We Kiss in a Shadow • and more.

00311558 ....$15.95

Country Love Songs – 4th Edition

This edition features 34 romantic country favorites: Amazed • Breathe • Could I Have This Dance • Forever and Ever, Amen • I Need You • The Keeper of the Stars • Love Can Build a Bridge • One Boy, One Girl • Stand by Me • This Kiss • Through the Years • Valentine • You Needed Me • more.

00311528 ....$14.95

The Definitive Love Collection – 2nd Edition

100 romantic favorites – all in one convenient collection! Includes: All I Ask of You • Can't Help Falling in Love • Endless Love • The Glory of Love • Have I Told You Lately • Heart and Soul • Lady in Red • Love Me Tender • My Romance • So in Love • Somewhere Out There • Unforgettable • Up Where We Belong • When I Fall in Love • and more!

00311681 ....$24.95

I Will Be Here

Over two dozen romantic selections from top contemporary Christian artists such as Susan Ashton, Avalon, Steven Curtis Chapman, Twila Paris, Sonicflood, and others. Songs include: Answered Prayer • Beautiful in My Eyes • Celebrate You • For Always • Give Me Forever (I Do) • Go There with You • How Beautiful • Love Will Be Our Home • and more.

00306472 ....$17.95

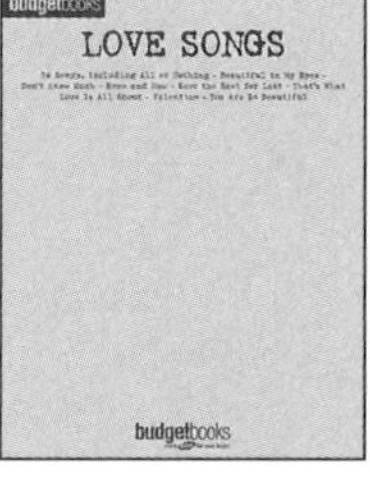

Love Songs

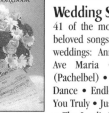

Budget Books Series

74 favorite love songs, including: And I Love Her • Cherish • Crazy • Endless Love • Fields of Gold • I Just Called to Say I Love You • I'll Be There • (You Make Me Feel Like) A Natural Woman • Wonderful Tonight • You Are So Beautiful • and more.

00310834 ....$12.95

The New Complete Wedding Songbook

41 of the most requested and beloved songs for romance and weddings: Anniversary Song • Ave Maria • Canon in D (Pachelbel) • Could I Have This Dance • Endless Love • I Love You Truly • Just the Way You Are • The Lord's Prayer • Through the Years • You Needed Me • Your Song • and more.

00309326 ....$12.95

New Ultimate Love and Wedding Songbook

This whopping songbook features 90 songs of devotion, including: The Anniversary Waltz • Can't Smile Without You • Could I Have This Dance • Endless Love • For All We Know • Forever and Ever, Amen • The Hawaiian Wedding Song • Here, There and Everywhere • I Only Have Eyes for You • Just the Way You Are • Longer • The Lord's Prayer • Love Me Tender • Misty • Somewhere • Sunrise, Sunset • Through the Years • Trumpet Voluntary • Your Song • and more.

00361445 ....$19.95

Romance – Boleros Favoritos

Features 48 Spanish and Latin American favorites: Aquellos Ojos Verdes • Bésame Mucho • El Reloj • Frenes • Inolvidable • La Vida Es Un Sueño • Perfidia • Siempre En Mi Corazón • Solamente Una Vez • more.

00310383 ....$16.95

Soulful Love Songs

Features 35 favorite romantic ballads, including: All My Life • Baby, Come to Me • Being with You • Endless Love • Hero • I Just Called to Say I Love You • I'll Make Love to You • I'm Still in Love with You • Killing Me Softly with His Song • My Cherie Amour • My Eyes Adored You • Oh Girl • On the Wings of Love • Overjoyed • Tonight, I Celebrate My Love • Vision of Love • You Are the Sunshine of My Life • You've Made Me So Very Happy • and more.

00310922 ....$14.95

Selections from

VH1's 100 Greatest Love Songs

Nearly 100 love songs chosen for their emotion. Includes: Always on My Mind • Baby, I Love Your Way • Careless Whisper • Endless Love • How Deep Is Your Love • I Got You Babe • If You Leave Me Now • Love Me Tender • My Heart Will Go On • Unchained Melody • You're Still the One • and dozens more!

00306506 ....$27.95

FOR MORE INFORMATION, SEE YOUR LOCAL MUSIC DEALER, OR WRITE TO:

7777 W. BLUEMOUND RD. P.O. BOX 13819 MILWAUKEE, WI 53213

www.halleonard.com

Prices, contents, and availability subject to change without notice.
Some products may not be available outside the U.S.A.

1004